Hanalei Colony Resort
A Special Place

George A. Ksander

Copyright © 2014 George A. Ksander
All rights reserved.

ISBN: 1500593060
ISBN-13: 9781500593063

Library of Congress Control Number: 2014913271
CreateSpace Independent Publishing Platform
North Charleston, South Carolina

Cover photos by Joe Jenkins/RezStream Inc.

To the People of
HCR,
Past, Present, and Future

Contents

Preface vii
Mahalo Nui Loa xi
Chapter 1 Arriving 1
Chapter 2 Wainiha 5
    Legends and History 7
    The Land: From Resource to Property 9
Chapter 3 Talk Story—Where It Is 21
Chapter 4 Ha'ena 29
    Tunnels 31
    Legends of the Caves 34
    Archeology, Legend, and History 36
    The Land: From Communal to Personal 38
    Taylor Camp 44
    Limahuli Garden 48
    Ke'e Beach 49
Chapter 5 Talk Story—What It Is 57
    Home 57
    Not Just an Investment 59
    A Place for Fun 60
    A Healing Hideaway 61
Chapter 6 A Place at the Beach 67
    Foundations 68
    Customizing 82
    Preserve and Protect 90
Chapter 7 Talk Story—How It Came to Be 99
Chapter 8 Life at the Beach 103
    The "Condo" 103

The "Resort"	108
A Destination	120
A Space Forever	132
Chapter 9 Talk Story—Coming Together	135
No Intent to Settle	136
Seeking	143
Like Attracts Like	146
The Final Resort	148
Onto the Generations	151
Chapter 10 Peril in Paradise	155
Unfriendly Water	156
Higher Than the Trees	158
A Strong and Piercing Wind	164
Chapter 11 Talk Story—The People	189
Guests	190
Friends and Neighbors	193
Family	199
Community	205
Chapter 12 A Special Place	213
Chapter 13 Departing	217
Glossary	219
Sources	223

Preface

This book is for the people of Hanalei Colony Resort (HCR)—owners, staff, neighbors, and guests past, present, and future. It is for HCR's *'ohana nui*, its extended family, its community. It tells of the big things that have shaped HCR, yet it also focuses on the small details of HCR: what it is, its history, how it works, what its people are like. If it brings a tear to an eye, stimulates a chuckle, jogs a memory, teaches something new, enables a new perception…if it kindles a desire to visit—or reignites a simmering desire—it will have been successful.

The intent of this book is to enable members of the community to share their own and their families' personal experiences at HCR and to expand their awareness of HCR's history and relationship to the surrounding area. If you are new to life at HCR, this book will introduce you to its rich history and, I hope, spark in you the desire to become part of its community.

First, in writing this book, I have attempted to capture and express the experiences of the HCR community, to show what it is like to be part of HCR and, thus, to enrich the unique experience of each individual with the shared experience of many. Second, I have tried to provide a picture of HCR in the wider setting of its location and its past, thereby enhancing the HCR experience by revealing the resort's deep historical connections to the north shore, to Kaua'i, and to Hawai'i. Third, I have presented the occasional peek behind the scenes at HCR. Ultimately the book combines these three approaches into a single, unified whole that is the HCR experience. Some themes will emerge: natural beauty; HCR as home, vacation spot, and retreat; links with the past; the lure of the place; friends, family, and community. My hope is that this book will serve as a kind of communal scrapbook.

During interviews, HCR's owners, staff, and neighbors shared personal experiences of life at the colony, memories of events and people, and perceptions of the surroundings. In some cases, I clarified information in interviews through follow-up e-mails and conversations. I collected guest experiences from comments left in the visitors' books that many owners provide when they rent out their units. Facts pertaining to the history of HCR and its operations came from interviews with many of the participants, along with documents and photographs they have contributed, and also from historical documents, including the minutes, planning materials, and official communications that are stored in HCR's own archives. I obtained some specific information about HCR from official county and state offices and gained additional context from newspaper and magazine stories and from historical collections archived by the Kaua'i Historical Society and the Kaua'i Museum. I derived more general information about HCR's setting in time and place from published books, popular and academic journals, and specialized websites. I included these in the list of sources at the back of the book.

In this book, we will first take a drive through Wainiha and Ha'ena to explore local sites of particular prominence in HCR's history. Then we shall focus in on HCR itself in order to get a sense of how it was born and developed and what it is like to be part of this little village. We will also replay a few events that occurred when HCR's setting and climate became noticeably more exciting and threatening. Along the way, we will occasionally sit down with various HCR folks to see what they see and hear what they have to say about HCR. Taken together, these disparate elements will help us better appreciate what HCR is and how it got that way.

This book documents the personal memories of many people, and, as such, these memories may differ from one another or from historical fact. Each individual went through a different experience and had access to different sources of information. The recorded memories represent the experiences of each person. I have not tried to rationalize the differences among them.

The book represents history as best as we can put it together. It is certainly incomplete, and it probably contains errors. I have used my best judgment to interpret the materials and to resolve discrepancies.

As you read the text, please note the following: Hawaiian words are italicized, except for common nouns and the names of people, organizations, and places that have become incorporated into English. Hawaiian equivalents for English words and English equivalents for Hawaiian words are given in parentheses when they first occur (or nearby) and are also listed in the glossary at the back of the book. I have included the names of many people throughout the text; each person's role at HCR—owner, staff, neighbor—has been identified in the acknowledgments section or, as I call it, *Mahalo Nui Loa*, that is, *Thank You Very Much* in Hawaiian.

Mahalo Nui Loa

At its core, this book is about people, so it is appropriate that many people have contributed to it. To all these, *mahalo nui loa*—"thank you very much." Laura Richards and Tom Stansell first conceived the idea of creating this history of HCR and talked me into getting involved. The managers of HCR Associates LLC provided support and ongoing encouragement. Much of the content has come directly from interviews with HCR owners and their family members: John Brekke, Marion Burns, Alicia Cortrite, Bob Eckert, Janne Hayward, Bob Johnstone, Averil and Howard Koch, Molly Ksander, Mary McGregor, Lionel Medeiros, Pat Montague, Dick Moody, Owen Paepke, Aggie Parlee, Cindy Ritter, Nancee and Rich Sells, Susan Shawgo, Dennie and Tom Stansell, Linda and Darrel Stoskopf, Carol and Jim Thompson, Claire Walker, Moreen and Chuck Williams, and Carl Woodbury; HCR staff, including Brandon Anakalea, Georgia Henry, Debra Jason, Royce "Cissie" Meyer, Laura and Tommy Richards, Joe Shannon, and Leland Swenson; and a neighbor, William Stewart. In addition to their memories, these folks graciously contributed their time, often on more than one occasion, for interviews, follow-up conversations, and e-mails. Regretfully, it was not possible to speak with every member of the HCR community. This list of interviewees is based as much on opportunity as on a systematic plan, but it is representative of owners and staff.

Special thanks go to Debra Jason and Linda Stoskopf for conducting some of the interviews and to Cathy Fiorelli for transcribing some. Tom Stansell introduced me to Marion Burns, and Rich Sells introduced me to Georgia Henry, thereby giving me access to information that otherwise would not have been available and would have been sorely missed. Of special note is that Dennie Stansell introduced me to the mysteries of the Tiki Goddess Cult.

Thank you also goes to all of the guests who have stayed at HCR and contributed to the community through their thoughtful and expressive writings in the guest books that owners provide in each apartment.

Marion Burns, Bob Eckert, Janne Hayward, Bob Johnstone, Mary McGregor, Susan Shawgo, Rich Sells, and Carl Woodbury have contributed photographs and documentary materials. Carl also contributed material from his own research on land history in the Kaua'i County tax records and the Kaua'i Museum. Jessi Anderson helped locate and transport multiple stashes of dusty HCR archives, some from a remote location, so that I could conveniently rummage through them and capture their hidden treasures. She also fielded a number of follow-up questions. Chris Faye, curator of collections at the Kaua'i Museum, and Mary Requilman, executive director of the Kaua'i Historical Society, were very helpful in steering me toward informative documents and making old photographs available. John Kruse and the office staff at the County Real Property Office in Lihue went out of their way to help me find precise maps of our area, which helped me resolve questions and illustrate points of history.

Bob Eckert, Janne Hayward, Joseph Ksander, Molly Ksander, and Rich Sells contributed greatly to the accuracy and readability of the book through their valuable comments on early drafts, in some cases on multiple drafts. These reviewers often provided just the right word to make the text come together. I am grateful to Candy Aluli and John Wehrheim for their coaching about approaches to editing. Candy also very graciously copyedited an intermediate draft, helpfully bringing my grammatical skills into the modern age. Alicia Cortrite and Bob Eckert provided professional help in addressing intellectual property issues. Michael Carlsson helped with business arrangements. Candy Aluli and Laura Richards helped with selecting and obtaining illustrations for the cover. I am also grateful to the very professional and helpful team at CreateSpace.

Janne Hayward, HCR's semiofficial historian, deserves special mention for her ongoing contributions throughout the project. Her long-term interest in HCR history, along with her own historical archives, enabled her to contribute specific documentation that helped to resolve questions about details of HCR's construction and operation and to clarify the presentation. I also greatly appreciated her continuing encouragement.

Finally, completion of this book has been made much easier as a result of the warm encouragement and guidance I have received from my listeners at various public readings of the draft text. These listeners have provided some unexpected and intriguing details and anecdotes. The response has reassured me that the book will be by and for the HCR community.

Chapter 1

Arriving

In the middle of the Pacific Ocean, on an island about as far from any mainland as you can get, on a beach on the far north shore, almost at the end of the road, seven one-lane bridges past the nearest town, waits a special place that is unspoiled, unplugged, unforgettable.

You are getting closer…following the narrow, twisting road on the cliff above the sea. You pass the last blind curve, and there it is, across the bay, waiting. You are here.

From the county road lined with tree-high red hibiscus, you enter the parking lot behind the resort. The lot is framed on your left by the towering thin triangles of Cook pines punctuated with overarching ironwoods and on your right by spreading false kamani trees speckled with scattered red leaves. There are coconut palms down the middle. Ahead, across the lot and beyond the naupaka hedges, you glimpse the Pacific Ocean. The smell of the sea permeates your soul. You enter through a little one-story cottage, which houses the office and reception area. Then you proceed to your dwelling. This will be one of fifty-two apartments spread around the resort in thirteen two-story wooden buildings surrounded by plantings of green ti and variegated croton and spider lilies—everywhere spider lilies. Many of the buildings circle a large lawn, a village green that funnels down to the beach and is framed by towering ironwood trees. Others arc around behind, spreading along a stream or reaching to the far end of the beach. A brilliant white egret lifts slowly off the ironwood hedge and glides off, out of sight. The footpaths lie behind the buildings, winding under scattered palm, plumeria, and kamani trees so that as you approach your apartment, you get a hint of what is coming. Then, from the back door, you pass through the narrow entryway into the open living room. You are drawn to the wide picture window and beyond: to the lanai and to the blue spreading ocean or the green misty mountains. The trade winds blow you away.

When your senses have relaxed after this feast, you wander through the grounds. The air is soft and warm. It brings you the scent of plumeria and Tahitian gardenia. Folks are motionless on lounge chairs—reading, napping, or just meditating on the soothing sounds of the surf. Or they are watching the kids play in the pool across the stream. There may be a single couple on the beach, hunting shells, or a net fisherman in tabis, stalking prey on the reef. Perhaps you glimpse a wedding party on the beach, its members decked in leis and holding hands. As dinnertime approaches, there will be the smell of barbecuing in progress and a glimpse of pupu platters on lanais. Inspired by this panorama, you stroll into the restaurant overlooking the beach, where you attend a Mai Tai Party to "talk story" (more about this custom in the next chapter) with other residents, guests, and staff and then stay on for a gourmet dinner. Or perhaps it is lu'au (feast) night. Sated and sleepy, you pause on the beach to watch the full moon rise out of the sea and pave a silvery road from the far horizon to your feet.

You think to yourself: Why is this place so special?

You are on the north shore of Kaua'i, at Kepuhi Point in the ahupua'a of Wainiha. You are at Hanalei Colony Resort (HCR). HCR is special because of where it is, what it is, and how it came to be. It is also special because of its people—who they are, how they came together, and how they have given life to HCR.

So exactly where is this special place?

Many people, locals and visitors alike, talk about HCR as being in Ha'ena, and think of Ha'ena as everything roughly from the Wainiha General Store out to Ke'e Beach at Ha'ena State Park; however, traditionally, the land where HCR is located has been considered part of Wainiha—more specifically, part of the Wainiha *ahupua'a*. HCR's founding documents do, in fact, locate it in Wainiha, "approximately one (1) mile from Ha'ena."

What is an *ahupua'a*? *Ahupua'a* is the word for a traditional Hawaiian unit of land. In general, an *ahupua'a* is the watershed associated with a stream running from a central highland down to the seashore; roughly speaking, it is a river valley. An *ahupua'a* provides all of the resources needed for its inhabitants to live, and everyone living in it accepts responsibility for maintaining those resources. Historically, the *ahupua'a* would provide fiber, gourds, sweet potatoes, and medicine; wood from trees in the interior mountains; bananas and sugar cane in the uplands; pili grass for thatch; taro ponds (*lo'i*) along the descending stream; and fish, shrimp, and seaweed along the shore. Hanalei is an *ahupua'a*. In our area, the traditional *ahupua'a* beyond Hanalei are Wai'oli, Waipa, Waikoko, Lumaha'i, Wainiha, and Ha'ena. Beyond Ha'ena, in Na Pali, the next *ahupua'a* is Hanakapi'ai.

Our continued usage of these names demonstrates how natural and useful the idea of an *ahupua'a* is. Throughout the Islands today, the idea of the *ahupua'a* is increasingly being used to guide residents in thinking about the best use of resources. The May/June 2013 edition of *Hawai'i* magazine reports that "the tenets of *ahupua'a* are finding modern-day supporters" and describes a number of projects aimed at promoting awareness and stewardship of these resources. In our area, the Waipa Foundation, with its native plant nursery and its weekly farmers' market, is one such project.

Prior to the colonization of the Islands by Europeans, all land was held in the name of the high chief (*ali'i nui*), who administered it on behalf of all the people. He delegated responsibility for an individual *ahupua'a* to a local chief (*ali'i'ai ahupua'a*), who administered it on behalf of the local residents as well as the principal chief. In large part, administration was concerned with management of local resources. All residents had access to common resources and shared the responsibility of maintaining these. They also had personal use of small parcels of land within the common space. These *kuleana* were house lots, personal taro ponds, cultivated patches of dry land, or particular patches of wild plants. The people were not tied to the land and would move from one *ahupua'a* to another if the local chief did not fulfill his role in a satisfactory manner.

Legends and folktales give us a sense of how people lived. They tell of bird catchers, foresters, fishermen, farmers, healers, lei (necklace, usually of flowers) makers, octopus hunters, *tapa* (cloth from mulberry plant) makers, warriors, dancers, kahunas (priests, experts), and managers. There are stories of both sedentary people and mobile ones, of small villages and isolated family units, of residences high in the mountains, deep in the valleys, and at the edge of the sea.

HCR is part of the Wainiha *ahupua'a*, and Wainiha has long been closely tied to Ha'ena. Therefore, the HCR community has deep ties to both Wainiha and Ha'ena. During your stay with us, we shall visit them both to see how HCR came to be. This history illustrates the direct links between HCR at the present moment and the life of ancient Hawai'i. This knowledge expands our community and enriches our shared experiences.

Chapter 2
Wainiha

You traverse a ridge on the winding road—a wooded cliff face on the left, the ocean on the right—and descend into the valley. You cross a small stream, with a bay to your right, and beyond a sandbar, the sea. There is a tiny village here—a few houses, a couple of shops. You press left around another curve and sense the depth of the valley. You stop to search carefully for any oncoming traffic before attempting the blind corner of the one-lane double bridge over the stream. Inland, the towering wall of the valley rises high above you. Safely across, you ascend again up the next ridge and squeak around a narrow blind curve. You have crossed the valley and entered onto a flat plain. The ridge now drops away to your left. Over there, to your right, on the point above the beach, is HCR. The road is straight here, and houses are scattered left and right. You have now glimpsed both faces of Wainiha: the valley and the plain.

Wainiha is narrow at the shoreline and penetrates deeply inland to the center of the island. Wainiha Valley is one of the longest and deepest river valleys on Kaua'i. It flows from Mount Wai'ale'ale at the top of the island and helps to drain the Alaka'i Swamp. Until the early days of western contact and colonization of the island, nine villages were scattered along its length. Ruins of house lots, taro patches, irrigation canals, and other engineering works can be found in the back of the valley and on down to the sea. Farthest up the valley was La'au (ridge), near a forest of wild bananas. Farther down, near the ridge that today's maps still call Maunahina (gray mountain), was a village of the same name. This was the beginning of the path up the ridge to Kilohana (lookout) in the

Alaka'i Swamp, the direct way to travel from the north shore through the swamp and Koke'e to Waimea. Maunahina was famous for the mokihana plants that grew there. Midway up the valley, close to the current power station, was the village Maunaloa (long mountain); at the mouth of the river, near today's Wainiha General Store, was the village of Pa'ie'ie (taro enclosure).

Wainiha Bay, 1906, looking west. Little vegetation is present. The wharf on the shoreline sandbar was built in 1906 for the Wainiha Powerhouse Project and was destroyed by the 1946 tsunami. Two houses are visible near the beach. Kepuhi Point is at the right, with one structure present. (Courtesy Kaua'i Museum)

Because various necessary resources were scarce in some places, the boundaries of an *ahupua'a* could be adjusted to compensate. This was the case in Wainiha. Because the river often flooded (in fact, the word *wainiha* means "angry, hostile, or unfriendly water"), the sea in Wainiha Bay was rough, and the shoreline was short, fish and other ocean resources were limited. Therefore, according to Frederick B. Wichman in his book *Kaua'i: Ancient Place-Names and Their Stories*, long before historic times, the residents and their ali'i extended the boundary of the Wainiha *ahupua'a* westward to include part of what otherwise would have been included in the Ha'ena *ahupua'a*. Carlos Andrade, in *Ha'ena: Through the Eyes of the Ancestors*, tells us that the boundary was finally settled in the mid-nineteenth century during the *Mahele* (see below) as the result of a dispute between the two ali'i who had been awarded Ha'ena and Wainiha. At the shore, the boundary between Wainiha and Haʻena is about where Naue, the YMCA camp, is presently located. In fact, the traditional name for the whole beachfront area, from the black lava tongue at the curve of the present road on the east to the Haʻena border on the west, was Naue, which means "trembling."

Legends and History

The flat land of Naue (sometimes misspelled as *Nane* in historical records) has long been noted for its prominent groves of hala (pandanus) trees; in fact, in 1888, J. Kahinu celebrated its beauty in a song he wrote called "Na Hala O Naue" (The Hala of Naue). Winds were strong, and the sea swept over the whole flat area from time to time, so it is believed that the people built only temporary working structures along the beach. Two streams, called Mene (dull, blunt) and Laukalo (taro leaf), ran through Naue.

The dwellers in Wainiha are mentioned frequently in legend and history. It is said that Wainiha was home to the Menehune and Mu people. Legend says that the Menehune were a tribe of native people who lived in remote areas of Kauaʻi. They were short in stature—two to four feet tall according to most sources, but as small as a mere six inches tall in some accounts—and very muscular. They were skilled craftsmen and were recruited for major public engineering projects such as the Alekoko Fishpond near Lihue and the Menehune Ditch at Waimea. Most interestingly, the Menehune performed all of their work at night. If they didn't finish in one night, the project would never be completed. The Menehune were also said to help humans who were in trouble. The Mu were a related tribe of ancient people, also of small stature, who were most famous for eating bananas.

The Menehune and the Mu may be a cultural memory of the first wave of Polynesian settlers from the Marquesas Islands, who arrived possibly as early as the eighth century AD, well before the settlers from the Society Islands, principally Tahiti and Raiatea, who arrived around the eleventh and twelfth centuries and soon dominated the Islands. A census conducted in 1800, soon after Europeans first arrived in the Islands, recorded sixty-five Menehune living in the depths of the valley at La'au. Around 1900, one resident of the valley claimed that his grandparents had been friendly with Menehune.

In his book *Kaua'i: Ancient Place-Names and Their Stories*, author Frederick Wichman tells a story about a woman who was teased because of some disfiguring birthmarks. One day, she was beating her kapa (a variant of tapa, or cloth from the mulberry plant) in Ka'aluhe'e Stream, on the east side of Wainiha, when a deep ocean octopus swam up and began to watch her. Remarkably, the coloring of the octopus was the same as the girl's birthmark. Because she was lonely, she began to talk to the octopus, which eventually revealed that he was a demigod who could appear as a man. He did so, and the two dallied in the stream. Due to the dalliance, she spoiled her kapa. Her parents tried to separate the pair, so the girl jumped off a cliff. Fortunately, she was changed into an octopus, and the two lovers were united forever. Wainiha is a place of romance.

Doug and Sandy McMaster have recorded a slack key guitar piece, "Pua Wainiha," which is named after a flower (*pua*) that is unique to the valley and commemorates a powerful *mo'o* (dragon or water spirit) goddess who lives in the valley and protects it.

The plains at Naue also feature in the epic story of Hi'iaka's journey to fetch the Kaua'i ali'i (chief) Lohi'au for her sister, the volcano goddess Pele, Lohi'au's lover, who was living in Kilauea Volcano on the Big Island. A cripple who was fishing recognized Hi'iaka and prepared a feast for her, during which he led the chanting of a song recounting Pele's story. Hi'iaka was so delighted that she restored the fisherman's ability to walk; thus, Wainiha is also a place for healing.

Archeological evidence suggests that people were living near the sea in Wainiha in about AD 750. In 1800, the konohiki, or manager, of the Wainiha *ahupua'a* under principal chief Kaumuali'i conducted a census of the valley and counted two thousand people. Because this figure included the sixty-five Menehune, it may be considered an approximation. The census count was down to 154 in 1847. The 2010 census counted 318 people in Wainiha, but this figure does not include the plain of Naue, which is now counted as part of Ha'ena. Peter Apo has commemorated this history of life in Wainiha with a line in his 1988 song "North Kaua'i Tapestry" recorded with Del Beazley.

For more than 125 years, the social and business center of Wainiha has been the Wainiha General Store. In the mid-nineteenth century, the church and school were located near the store. An 1891 notice in the *Hawaiian Gazette* reported that A. N. K. Kapohaku had purchased the "DRY GOODS STORE known as the WAINIHA STORE." Sometime before 1916, the store was acquired by the Nakatsuji family and became known as the Nakatsuji Store until the late twentieth century. Since the mid-1970s, the store has been owned and operated by Janet Mello and her family. In 2014, Janet retired, and her son has carried on running the store, while her daughter manages the adjacent food stand and gallery.

In 1918, Prince Kuhio, the Hawaiian territorial delegate to the US Congress, met with his local constituents in front of the Nakatsuji Store. The blog *Wainiha Nation* often describes events centered around the Wainiha General Store, but many of these should probably be taken as fantasy rather than history. There was a gas pump at the Wainiha General Store as recently as 1969. H. Young, an artist who lived right by the store, documents this in a 1969 oil painting. David Ballard, Mary McGregor's husband, commissioned Young to paint "this house, this bridge, this store, and this old rusty gas pump. We have to have a picture of this thing." Dave traded their Volkswagen camper for the painting. The artist and his girlfriend then went off to the Big Island to live in it. Mary has the painting proudly displayed on the wall of her apartment at HCR.

The Land: From Resource to Property

Ownership of land at HCR is derived from the Hawaiian monarchy. How this came about is an instructive story that directly links King Kamehameha III, the *Mahele*, the formation of an early homeowners' association, twentieth-century courtroom proceedings, and contemporary real estate transactions.

After Kamehameha I unified the Islands into a single kingdom, the principal chief was called the king (*mo'i* in Hawaiian). He nominally held all of the land. Beginning in 1846, King Kamehameha III began a legal process that would distribute the lands among the king, the nobles (the *ali'i*, or the lower chiefs, and their families), and the people (*maka'ainana* or *hoa'aina*). This process was called the *Mahele*. Whole *ahupua'a* were awarded to high chiefs, and smaller parcels of land, called *kuleana*, within the *ahupua'a* were awarded to individuals who could establish that they had lived and worked on those parcels. The *Mahele* introduced private ownership of land to Hawai'i and, especially, brought land ownership to ordinary people living on it. The impact of the *Mahele* is expressed in the wording of the present-day deeds of ownership of residential units at HCR. In a sense, owners at HCR received their property originally as a gift from King Kamehameha III, Kauikeaouli.

In the *Mahele*, Mikahela Kekauonohi was granted the entire *ahupua'a* of Wainiha. M. Kekauonohi was a high chiefess of Maui and the granddaughter of Kamehameha I. She participated in the battle at the Russian Fort Elizabeth at Waimea in 1824, on the side of the Oahu forces, and she served as governess of Kaua'i from 1840 to 1845. Wainiha was one of about twenty-nine *ahupua'a* that she was awarded throughout the Islands, along with some other smaller parcels. She received more land than anyone aside from the king. Today, the deeds to dwelling units at HCR refer to Land Commission Award (LCA) 11216:5. The Land Commission was the government office set up in 1846 to administer disputes about the distribution of lands in the *Mahele*. LCA 11216:5 refers to the award of the *ahupua'a* of Wainiha to Mikahela Kekauonohi in 1853. After the Land Commission awarded a parcel of land to an individual, the award was formalized when the king granted a Royal Patent (RP) to the land. M. Kekauonohi received RP 7194 for Wainiha.

In 1842, a man named Naauole was given some smaller plots of land, or *kuleana*, within Wainiha by his parents, who had lived there since about 1829. These *kuleana* were essentially personal, private property. Naauole's property included a house lot and four adjoining patches of taro ponds and dry, open fields called *kula*. He lived on and cultivated these plots until 1849, when he went to sea. In the *Mahele*, Naauole was awarded these *kuleana* in LCA 10334:1 and 2, and these awards were confirmed with Royal Patent Number 6960, which is mentioned in HCR deeds. Naauole's land is the site of present-day HCR. In particular, in his testimony to the Land Commission, Naauole mentioned that the lot where his house was located was bounded by the sea beach on one side and the stream Mene on the other. It is likely that this stream is the stream that runs through HCR today.

The Land Commission made similar *kuleana* awards of house lots, taro patches, and *kula* to approximately forty other people throughout Wainiha. People continued to live and work the land in Wainiha, although there is evidence that occupation became more concentrated closer to the sea rather than higher up the valley. The rest of the *ahupua'a* land that had not been awarded to individuals as *kuleana* was still held by M. Kekauonohi at her death in 1851. According to a scholar of Hawaiian land history, Lilikala Kame'eleihiwa, and the archeologists Kekapala P. Dye and T. S. Dye, Wainiha passed to Kekauonohi's husband, Levi Ha'alelea, at her death. When Ha'alelea died in 1864, his lands were sold to pay his debts. In 1866, J. H. Morse, John de Fries, and J. Halstead bought Wainiha at auction for $3,200. In 1871, De Fries sold his share to Castle & Cooke, one of the "Big Five" companies that dominated Hawaiian commerce and agriculture in the nineteenth century (and is now a major property developer throughout the Islands and US mainland). When Morse died, she left her shares to Castle & Cooke in trust to sell. Finally, in 1877, the *Hui Ku'ai 'Aina O Wainiha*, acting through its agent J. Leka (or perhaps T. Leka), purchased Wainiha from Castle & Cooke. According to Carlos Andrade, the handwritten bylaws of the hui state that it paid $5,500, and that it had been making payments since 1869.

The *Hui Ku'ai 'Aina O Wainiha* (which translates as the "Group to Purchase the Land of Wainiha") or the Wainiha Hui, as it was commonly called, is an example of what became a new way of organizing land ownership and usage. Similar organizations occurred elsewhere on Kaua'i, as we shall see, and throughout the Islands. The hui was created in 1877, when seventy-one owners of individual *kuleana* within Wainiha legally joined together in an organization to purchase and manage the common lands of Wainiha. This was essentially the first homeowners' association in Wainiha. It had directors, officers, an office, and an annual meeting held at the Hui Hall, which was located "on the beach at Wainiha," according to the *Garden Island*. Individual owners had voting rights. A resident manager (*luna nui,* or "high overseer") and executive committee managed the affairs of the hui, including its debt and property taxes.

The Wainiha Hui communally owned about fifteen thousand acres of Wainiha Valley. In addition to access to the common lands and resources, each member received personal use of five acres of arable dry land, mauka (inland), and five acres of arable wetland, makai (seaward). These were selected by the individual members and approved by the manager. In addition to each resident's personal *kuleana,* members of the hui also enjoyed access, essentially an easement, to common resources throughout the *ahupua'a.* The land was never formally surveyed and divided up, so some disputes occurred. Newspaper articles frequently mention that discussions about the distribution of hui lands occupied much of the annual meetings. These were settled by an executive committee of the hui. Apparently, the course of meetings was similar to that of homeowners' associations today. In 1911, the *Garden Island* reported that at the recent annual meeting, a question arose: Who owned the 'awa (pepper plant used for ceremonial drink) growing in the mountains: the man who planted it, the hui, or the Lord? As the newspaper documented, "The question became more uncertain the longer it was discussed. And was finally turned over to the directors to settle."

The Reverend John M. Lydgate, in the 1913 edition of the *Hawaiian Almanac and Annual,* told a more colorful—but probably inaccurate—story of the formation of the Wainiha Hui. According to Lydgate, one way to make big money at this time was to collect sandalwood from the native forests and sell it in China, where it was highly valued for use in precious wood chests, perfume, and ceremonies. Hawaiian sandalwood traders built large fortunes. In this version, Kekauonohi mortgaged the Wainiha property to Aldrich and Company of Queen Street in Honolulu for $10,000 in order to finance a shipment of sandalwood to Shanghai. (To the extent that Aldrich and Company may have been involved in the financial affairs of Wainiha, this story illustrates another deep historic connection between Wainiha and Ha'ena. Aldrich and Company became the Bank of Bishop & Co. Ltd, named after Charles Reed Bishop, the husband of Princess Bernice Pauahi Bishop, and then evolved into today's First Hawaiian bank. As we shall see in Chapter 4, Princess Bernice Pauahi Bishop once owned the Ha'ena *Ahupua'a*.) Kekauonohi used the residents in Wainiha to harvest the sandalwood from far up in the valley and bring it down to be loaded on the schooner *Manu-o-ka-wai* (Bird of the Water). The ship and its load of valuable sandalwood then disappeared without a trace. The anticipated profits were lost along with the ship. Kekauonohi was able to pay back $1,000 of the money owed to Aldrich and Company but still needed $9,000 more.

So Kekauonohi developed a creative plan to convert the Wainiha land into the needed money. Kekauonohi convinced the Wainiha residents to pool their money so that they might jointly buy out the remainder of the *ahupua'a*. Ninety residents would each contribute one hundred dollars toward the total. Local leaders campaigned hard to enable the plan. The one-hundred-dollar investments were obtained in a variety of ways. Some residents signed on to work on the new sugar plantation at Hanalei and took an advance on a year's wages. Some mortgaged their individual *kuleana* and then worked off the debt. Others gave a promissory note for their piece of the new communal land, using all of their possessions as collateral. Eventually seventy-one residents paid in their shares. This yielded a total of only $7,100, short of the needed $9,000. Through negotiation among Kekauonohi, the local representatives of the residents, and Aldrich and Company, a scheme was worked out whereby Aldrich would accept the $7,100 and the residents would commit to paying off the remaining $2,000 at 15 percent interest.

Unfortunately, this version of the formation of the Wainiha Hui is probably fanciful, perhaps based on folklore that Lydgate heard while serving as a surveyor for the Wainiha power line project around 1904. As suggested by the archeologists Kekapala P. Dye and T. S. Dye, problems with Lydgate's version include the fact that Kekauonohi died in 1851, twenty-five years before the Wainiha Hui was formed; that the sandalwood trade had collapsed in the 1840s; and that the schooner *Manu-o-ka-wai* was not lost at sea but was still sailing the interisland route in 1883. The true story is more prosaic, but Lydgate's version may contain seeds of the truth that suggest how individual members may have financed the hui.

The business affairs of the Wainiha Hui apparently did not prosper. Taxes were an issue. The crops yielded little or no profit. Shares lost value. According to the *Maui News*, "It was often a problem how their taxes were to be paid." The *luna nui* was authorized to levy an assessment to pay taxes. The *Hawaiian Annual* for 1924 reported that when a meeting of the hui was called to discuss a proposal to lease water rights, word spread that it was "not to raise money, nor anything about taxes!" and that meetings always meant "fresh pilikia [trouble], some fresh demand for money."

Wainiha Valley, 1924. A few structures are visible among the trees along the road in the foreground, scattered in the valley, and along Powerhouse Road. The double bridge can be seen crossing the stream, and the Wainiha wharf is visible in the foreground. (Courtesy of the Kaua'i Museum)

The hui's financial situation improved around 1905. Sugar production required water, and water required power for pumping. Then, as now, the need for electric power on Kaua'i required importation of fuel—then coal, now oil. McBryde Sugar Company was a large operation on the south shore that had been formed by uniting several smaller companies, including the Koloa Plantation, which was the first sugar plantation in the Hawaiian Islands. To reduce the cost of electricity, McBryde formed a division named Kaua'i Electric to construct a hydroelectric plant up the Wainiha Stream that would provide cheaper power for its operations at 'Ele'ele on the south side of the island. To enable this, McBryde proposed to lease water rights and land for the power facility from the Wainiha Hui for fifty years. The hui would receive a dividend of $1,500 per year. Following two special meetings (probably held on property close to where HCR is located today) to discuss the pros and cons of McBryde's proposal, the members of the Wainiha Hui approved the proposal and authorized the officers of the hui to sign the lease. Powerhouse Road, by the double bridge over the Wainiha stream, was so named because it is the access road to the hydroelectric facility. A wharf was constructed at the beach, and a temporary railroad was laid up the valley to support construction of the facility. (The wharf was destroyed in the 1946 tsunami.) The powerhouse and distribution line were dedicated in 1905. Today, the powerhouse is just visible at the end of Powerhouse Road, and part of the distribution line is accessible via the hiking path along the Powerline Trail from Princeville to the Keahua Arboretum above Wailua.

Earlier, members had been assessed to pay the hui's taxes, but hui residents now received a portion of the income from the power company. In 1908, the *Maui News* reported that the hui was so "opulent" as a result of the lease that members received a dividend of fourteen dollars per share. In 1919, it was fifteen dollars per share. The *Garden Island* reported that in 1919, individual "shares are worth five or six times what they were before the deal was made." Members of the hui sometimes sold their *kuleana* to buyers who were not residents of the *ahupua'a*. The *Garden Island* claimed that, by 1919, more than half of the shares "drifted into the hands of three or four interested parties, the chief of which naturally is the Kaua'i Electric Co." As part of the water rights lease agreement, McBryde Sugar Company also committed to holding a lu'au for the annual meeting of the hui members. This annual meeting was evidently quite an event for the whole island. This was largely "due to the publicity concerning the big spreads that usually follow," according to Lydgate. The *Garden Island* reported that island notables—such as W. H. Rice, G. N. Wilcox, C. Dole, and J. M. Lydgate, among others—attended the 1913 meeting.

The creation of the hydroelectric plant also served as the basis for the eventual creation of the Kaua'i Island Utility Cooperative (KIUC), which today provides electric power to the island. In the early 1950s, Kaua'i Electric merged with Lihue Plantation's Waiahi Electric Company. In 1969, Kaua'i Electric became a division of Citizens Utilities Company. In 1999, Kaua'i leaders formed KIUC, and in 2002, KIUC acquired Kaua'i Electric Company. In 2009, the Wainiha hydroelectric plant (by then owned by the Kaua'i Coffee Company, which had succeeded McBryde Sugar in 1987) provided 6 percent of the island's electricity. Here we see how major components of Kaua'i's contemporary economy trace back to the island's sugar plantation history, through the hui, and, eventually, to Wainiha's geologic setting.

Taro farmer's cottage in Wainiha, early twentieth century. (Courtesy Kaua'i Historical Society)

The hui also carried out other business ventures, such as exporting 'awa, a relaxing preparation of the local pepper plant that is used for medicine and rituals. Today kava, as it is more widely called, can be obtained from several commercial suppliers, but none of these are in Wainiha. Several hui members, notably the Robinson family, ran cattle in Wainiha. Originally, the beachfront land in Wainiha was wetland planted with taro. In the late 1800s, Chinese farmers took the lead in replacing taro cultivation with rice planting. The *Garden Island* reports that Kahei Haraguchi obtained permission from the Robinson family to plant rice in the area where HCR exists today. This is the same Haraguchi family that today operates the rice mill and taro farm tours, as well as the food stand in Hanalei. According to the *Garden Island*, this is the only restored working rice mill in the Islands.

Today, the Wainiha Valley is itself being preserved. In 2007, Alexander & Baldwin, the parent company of McBryde Sugar Company, signed a ten-year agreement with the Nature Conservancy to manage the pristine upper reaches of the valley, including portions of the Alaka'i Swamp and the Wai'ale'ale summit area. This area contains 127 species of flowering plants found only in Hawai'i and 41 species found only on Kaua'i, as well as numerous rare bird species. The shoreline of Wainiha is also being conserved. In 2008, a group of local landowners donated the parcel of beach land along the west side of Wainiha Bay to the Kaua'i Public Land Trust (which later became part of the Hawaiian Islands Land Trust). This group included family members of HCR owner Mary McGregor, who made the donation in Mary's honor.

HCR deeds describe the land as "portions of hui Lots 77-A and 76-B of the Wainiha Hui land." This designation refers to the dissolution of the Wainiha Hui. In 1947, McBryde Sugar Company initiated legal action to dissolve the Wainiha Hui. Over time, the value of shares had become diluted as members of the hui divided their shares among their children. In addition, many *kuleana* had been sold to people who were not original members of the hui, so that only seven shares were still held by heirs of the original hui members. McBryde had previously purchased forty-eight shares, and the Robinson brothers had bought sixteen shares. McBryde now wished to survey the land, pay off existing heirs and other members, and obtain clear title to all of the Wainiha Hui land. By this time, an original share of the hui was worth about $5,000. To complete the legal action to dissolve the hui, all of the heirs of the original members needed to be identified, and their interests had to be satisfied. Because of the long history of subdividing and selling shares, this was a vast and complicated job.

A commission (J. B. Corstorphine, R. Garlinghouse, and W. F. Sanborn) was formed to accomplish the dissolution. An advertisement aimed at locating these heirs ran in the *Garden Island* on March 5, 1946. Many of the heirs were unknown and were simply identified as "heir of Makanui," "heir of Kanohi," and so on. Eventually, all of the heirs were located and their interests satisfied. The hui lands were surveyed, divided up, identified by number and letter, and assigned to individual hui members in fee simple, meaning that the recipients fully owned the land rather than leasing it. The final decree dissolving the Wainiha Hui was filed on November 21, 1947. Among the members who received parcels of land were Jack N. and Ivy Nishimoto, who, between them, had about one full share of the original hui. The parcels received by the Nishimotos included Lot 76 and Lot 77 of the Wainiha Hui lands. As described in the HCR deeds, this is the land now occupied by HCR and the adjacent restaurant. Ivy Nishimoto was born near here and remembers growing up "like in the stories of old…grass shack, fish, taro, salt, hukilaus [community fishing events], and so forth," according to her website.

On contemporary maps, this area is shown as Kepuhi Point. One meaning of the word *puhi* is "blowhole." According to Leland Swenson and Brandon Anakalea, who both grew up in the vicinity of HCR, the name does refer to a small blowhole, which, when conditions are right, can be seen spouting from the black lava tongue at the eastern end of the beach below the sharp turn in the road. Kepuhi Point probably made its cinematic debut as the background for the opening credits of the 1950 Esther Williams film *Pagan Love Song*. The 2011 film *Soul Surfer* also includes a brief drive-by shot of Kepuhi Beach.

Blowhole at eastern end of Kepuhi Beach. (From the author's collection)

HCR is not the first collection of Euro-American structures near Kepuhi Point. Rich Sells has heard that during World War II, the US Marines constructed barracks for troops stationed at the point, and Mary McGregor, who was familiar with the owners of the land prior to construction of HCR, confirms this. The area may have been considered sensitive because of the need to secure the Wainiha powerhouse. The barracks were abandoned after the war. Later, the Nishimoto family operated the Motel Hale Hoomaha (House of Relaxation or House of Hospitality) at Kepuhi Point, "the present site of the Hanalei Colony Resort," according to Ivy Nishimoto's website. In 1957, the rate was six dollars a day for a couple. (A bed and breakfast of the same name currently operates nearby on Alamihi Road, but it is unrelated to the earlier motel.) The Nishimotos' motel may have utilized the surplus barracks;

however, according to Mary McGregor, the tsunami of 1946 destroyed all remnants of the barracks.

Hale Hoomaha itself was lost in the 1957 tsunami. The Nishimotos escaped by car after hearing a radio warning just five to ten minutes before the wave arrived. Following this event, which was the second tsunami to flood the motel, the Nishimotos moved farther up Wainiha Valley—"high enough up so that another tidal wave would not touch us again," says Ivy Nishimoto on her website. By the late 1960s, there was a scattering of houses near Kepuhi Point: two near the beach, three across the road just east of the future HCR, and one on the beach just to the west.

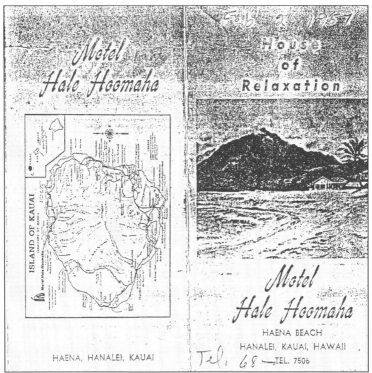

1957 brochure for Motel Hale Hoomaha.
(Courtesy Bob Johnstone)

Chapter 3

Talk Story—Where It Is

When HCR folk are sitting around chatting, shooting the breeze, cracking jokes, and exchanging anecdotes—what is called Talk Story in the Islands—some common themes, questions, and answers come up again and again. Whether folks are at Mai Tai Night, sitting on their lanai, or puttering around the barbecue—and the barbecue is very often the setting for these discussions—questions arise repeatedly as to just what it is about HCR that attracts and delights people.

A visitor to the north shore happens to notice HCR as she drives by on her way to see Ke'e Beach. On the way back, she stops to explore the grounds and becomes enchanted. In the office she is happily surprised to find that there is a vacancy for that night. She takes an apartment for the evening, and in her suite she finds an invitation to something called Mai Tai Night. So she heads to the restaurant and is met by a crowd of happy campers. She mixes into the conversation. At one point, she realizes that sprinkled among the guests at her table are several people who own apartments at HCR. She is excited at her good fortune. Now she can find out all about the place! "Oh," she says, "this place is wonderful; I am so lucky to have found it. What brings you all here? What is it about this place that attracts you?" HCR people never tire of describing the beauty and spirit of this place. Her hosts respond.

Fred Marotta writes in one of his president's letters:

> In Kaua'i, especially our north shore, it is easy to understand how the aloha spirit permeates the island and the people. Our piece of paradise has a special 'aina,

which seems to feed the soul. It does not matter what one's background, practically everyone who visits picks up on the intricate intertwining of this land and spirit. Whether it be a gentle caress of the wind, or the water playfully tossing you about, one cannot escape the power of the ʻaina. How many of you shed a tear or two upon leaving?

Again and again, owners, staff, and guests echo this sentiment and fill in the details.

"What do I love about it? I love everything," answers Howard Koch.

"The surfing opportunities, the peace and solitude, the location, and the beauty" are what Dick Moody loves, confirms his daughter Linda Stoskopf.

For Aggie Parlee, the attraction of HCR is the natural environment and its remoteness: "How many places do you go over eight one-lane bridges to get to? I don't know of a better place." Debra Jason agrees: "It's a sweet spot." Georgia Henry feels that "there's a vibe here that hits you the minute you walk on the property. It's very special. The minute you step on the property, there's just a big sigh: 'Oh thank God I'm here.'"

"It is a perfectly lovely location," asserts Owen Paepke. "Objectively, you will not find any places in the country that will rival it in terms of pure, simple, serenic—if that is a word—beauty. It is just an amazing combination of physical beauty and separation from all the hustle and bustle the world imposes on us every day."

"The ocean, the remoteness, the end of the road," says Molly Ksander. Then too, as Molly's daughter-in-law shouted out excitedly, grinning and running into the living room, "There are trade winds in the bathroom!"

"You really have to love HCR," says Darrel Stoskopf. "You have to go through one-lane bridges, on narrow roads. It's like you are going to a place that not many people have the privilege of going, and it is tropical; it is on the ocean. We love the ocean sounds, the breeze, and the people are friendly."

And William Stewart: "There's an energy here, a majestic feeling. You're just nestled in between these beautiful green majestic mountains, and this beautiful blue ocean. Everyone that comes out to the north shore of Kaua'i has a feeling that you're in touch with nature. It's just a mystical, magical feeling."

Guests concur. As one recorded, "We have no words to describe this island. It is paradise on earth."

Another guest's first impressions dramatically illustrate the unique setting of HCR:

> We drove in at night with the wind howling around our car and the rains heavily pounding the windshield. In the rainy darkness, tall tropical trees, vines cascading down, loomed around the twisting snakelike corners of the road to the end of the line—Hanalei Colony Resort. I half expected a glistening velociraptor to pop its head out from among the jungle brush. This definitely wasn't Waikiki Beach!

Unlike other resorts on the north shore, HCR is located on the edge of the ocean—where the land meets the sea. It is as close to the water as any resort on Kaua'i and closer than any other place on the north shore. For Darrel Stoskopf, "the ocean is a magnet." Carl Woodbury tells about the first time his family stayed at HCR. The first thing his daughter did was dash through the building to the ocean. "My daughter, Molly, would have been nine or ten," Carl recalls. "I remember her running back in from the deck, and she tells us, 'Dad, Mom, it's only ten Molly steps to the beach!'"

For Linda Stoskopf, "the water is so close, to me it is kind of like a homecoming, because that is how I grew up. Walk out the door and there is the ocean." Some owners and guests swim daily, within the reef just off the HCR beach; others may not swim every day, but they at least wade.

You cannot find a better place than HCR's beach to watch the rosy-fingered tendrils of dawn rise up out of the sea and transform, somehow, into the blinding silver glow of the newly risen sun.

A newcomer's first sight of HCR often occurs at dawn, and it is often emotional. Moreen Williams tells how the sight of HCR affected Chuck's sister on her first visit. She arrived at night, in the dark, and slept in the *pune'e* (movable couch) room:

> I get up in the morning. I'm out there drinking my coffee on the lanai and I hear the thing open up and she's going, "Oh my God!" And she comes running out in her nightgown and she says, "Oh my God! This is the most gorgeous thing I've ever seen." So, yeah, it's just a magical place; it truly is. And Puff does live here.

Sunrise at HCR is also one of Pat Montague's favorite things: "Getting up in the morning and getting a cup of coffee and sitting out there and watching the sun come up. I love sitting out there and just staring at the ocean. It's marvelous. I wish I could bring it home."

Guests as well as owners often comment on the sunrise. "As the sun rose this morning, its rays would shine and illuminate the spray off the tops of the eight-foot breakers. The spray looked like the manes of a thundering herd of wild horses pounding its way to shore," one visitor eloquently recorded in a guest book.

The passionate appreciation of HCR cannot be explained by naïveté or lack of experience on the part of its aficionados, because its people travel widely. Bob Eckert can quantify his comparison:

> At that point [in 1976] I had lived or worked in six countries. And had seen other countries in Africa, Europe, and Asia. And thirty-nine states of the United States. And the day I spent on the north shore in July of '76, I thought I had seen the most beautiful meeting of mountains and ocean that I had seen anywhere. That beauty that I discovered in 1976, and then have

enjoyed since '84, it's still here. Now they total sixty-eight countries.

Georgia Henry is emphatic: "I loved it then, and I love it now. There's no other place—and I've traveled extensively—there's no other place I'd rather return to than HCR." Moreen and Chuck Williams are another example, as Moreen reflects: "I mean, this is a magical place. We've been a lot of places in the world, but this is the most magical. We've been to Tahiti. We've been other places. I have to tell you, we think the beaches here are prettier than anywhere else we've ever been." Such broad geographical experience is common among the HCR community. So their appreciation has a solid foundation.

Bob Johnstone frequently spends time at the barbecue area because it provides an opportunity to mingle with guests and hear "what they liked and didn't like." He has often heard them sing the praises of Kaua'i and of HCR. "Many, many, many times people would say, 'We've been to Oahu; we've been to Maui; we came here last. We wish we would've come here first because we wouldn't have gone to those other places.' I've heard that countless times."

Haven't we all heard this again and again, read it in our guest books, and played it out ourselves? "We arrived in Kaua'i after having spent several days in Maui. Almost immediately we noticed how different the energy is between the two islands. There is a pervasive calm on this island," says a guest.

The attraction of HCR is partly the magnetism of the north shore. "The location, the environment. It is mellow; it is gorgeous. It is a very soothing place, and it happens to be at HCR," muses Linda Stoskopf. Cissie Meyer sees exactly this: "There's so many people that just fall in love with the place. 'The place' could be the Hanalei Colony Resort, or 'the place' could be the north shore and they happen to be staying at the resort. But there's no place like the resort on the north shore."

Here is Lionel Medeiros, who lives on the south shore but is also an HCR owner:

> I've only been off the island of Kaua'i once in seven years. If that doesn't make me island-happy, I don't know what the heck does. And the kids and the grandchildren love the place, too. They've stayed on the north shore and the south shore. They always prefer the north shore because it's so isolated. This is like heaven. It is different.

The beauty created by the distinctive interplay of mountain and sea is compelling for guests as well as owners. "Nothing beats the north shore of Kaua'i. It is probably one of the most breathtaking places on earth," says one guest. "The natural beauty comparable to the Alps, Rockies, and Grand Canyon, but with the incomparable sea to boot!" another says. An inspired guest turns HCR into poetry:

Surfing sunshine waves,
Cold coconut hot sand beach,
Billions of stars watching.

Above all else, HCR and its setting are prototypically Hawaiian. Chuck Williams describes it like this: "You know, it's laid back; it's what Hawai'i is all about. We've been to all the other Islands. Even this island on the south side has become very commercialized, and it's not here. Right here it's just what Hawai'i should be." John Brekke is of the same mind: "One of the things I love the most about here is the ocean, the beauty. It is just the setting. It's a sense of aloha here that's so terrific. I don't think I have one memory associated with HCR other than the spirit of the place. It's just great." Bob Johnstone feels the same spirit of nature:

> It's the location. We were used to places like the Hyatt, which are beautiful, but they're very man-made. We came up here. It was so peaceful, and the beauty is so natural. From Hanalei to Ke'e, it's all Hawai'i; it's probably as good as you're going to get it these days. There are stretches of the beach where you don't see anybody in either direction. You look both directions, you don't

see a single soul anywhere. Where else can you find that these days?

The experience of HCR includes its native wildlife. Cats patrol the grounds. You can watch whales from your lanai. There are ghost crabs on the beach, geckos on your stairs (or your walls, if you are blessed), frogs singing in the night, and a guidebook full of birds coming and going. Guests sometimes get to see turtles right out in front of the resort or an endangered Hawaiian monk seal on the beach, behind its protecting stakes and caution tape. One especially fortunate guest even reported seeing sea turtles and a monk seal at the same time! One time a goat named Eddie tried to register at the office before a staff member took it back up the hill to its own home pasture. Molly Ksander sadly misses the white horse that used to stand on an island in the Wainiha stream like a semimystical silent sentinel guarding the double bridge. And, of course, there have always been chickens.

Hawaiian monk seal on beach just west of HCR, 2007. (Courtesy Janne Hayward)

Kaua'i is such a prototypical example of Hawai'i that formal educational programs bring students to study its "biodiversity, evolution, island formation, and the spectacular nature of Hawai'i," as one guest who is a faculty member recorded. Indeed, one owner first experienced HCR as a graduate student attending a seminar here. A guest who grew up "down the road" in Ha'ena says that HCR has "much more of a *kama'aina* (native born) feel than the typical tourist hotel." Nancee Sells' explanation of why she and Rich wanted to become owners at HCR sums up this sense of the real Hawai'i: "It was remote; it was more like a tropical island than you can get anywhere else. It didn't have the big motel atmosphere. It really felt like you were stepping back into Hawaiiana."

As a visitor from the Big Island put it, "This is how Hawai'i is supposed to be. Let's keep it that way."

Look out your window or into your mind. What color is the sea at this moment? What is the sound of the sea? How do the mountains feel on your fingertips? What is in your mind's eye?

Chapter 4

Ha'ena

From HCR, you go west. At first you pass through the flatlands between pasture and sea, with dwellings all around and the ridges ahead of you, just visible above the trees. Here you cross a border into ancient Ha'ena. Soon you curve inland and descend to ford a small stream, and the sea is with you again—and the wind. You pass the dark, dry cave mouth (was that a shiver of apprehension?), curve round the beach, and climb one of those ridges. Now you are up against the cliff; the lush overgrowth blocks your view. There are no more buildings, but there are more caves in the cliff wall, beside you and above you. You sense a change in the air: something new. You cross an open space, rocky terraces ascending up the valley. You cross another stream, pass a taro field below, and enter a dark tunnel of trees curtained with long, leafy jungle vines. The trees thin out on your left, giving way to the looming cliff, and then—the end of the road! You walk the last few feet to the sand, to the light, to the blue lagoon and the cliffside glistening above. You have traversed Ha'ena.

HCR may be located in the Wainiha *ahupua'a*, but its past and present are seamlessly interwoven with that of Ha'ena. Prior to the growth of natural and man-made obstructions, Wainiha and Ha'ena were united visually. You could see from one to the other: from Kepuhi Point all the way to Maniniholo Dry Cave at what is now Ha'ena Beach County Park. There was continual travel back and forth for supplies and commercial business. Both areas were dependent on the Wainiha General Store for supplies. HCR staff and their families have long lived in Ha'ena. Ha'ena residents have had a continuing impact on HCR's history, from both a business and personal point of view. The two *ahupua'a* have been hand in hand through storm and wave. Perhaps most importantly, many of the HCR community's most memorable experiences have occurred in Ha'ena: in places such as Tunnels, the dry cave of Maniniholo, Limahuli Valley, and Ke'e Beach.

Ha'ena looking east from Ke'e Beach in foreground to Naue flats in the distance, 2008. (From the author's collection)

Where Wainiha is narrow and deep, Ha'ena is broad and shallow. The *ahupua'a* of Ha'ena (burning, red-hot; intense breath) stretches lengthwise from Naue at the ocean border with Wainiha to the far edge of Ke'e lagoon at the beginning of Na Pali. The western boundary runs along the ridge between the Limahuli and Hanakapi'ai Valleys. Ha'ena is mostly a strip of flat, sandy land along the coast, but it also includes a thin slice of the mountain terrain that extends inland from the coastal ridge. The cliffs are cut by a small stream valley, Manoa (vast, deep, thick), which opens to the sea at Ha'ena Beach County Park, and a much larger stream valley, Limahuli (turning hands), that extends deeper into the mountains. Today Manoa Valley is inaccessible. It is privately owned and so heavily overgrown that one might never know it is there. Limahuli Valley has appeared in several films, notably *Jurassic Park* (1993). A large part of Ha'ena is fronted by a long lagoon called Makua (ancestors), which is protected by a fringing reef called Papaloa (long reef) and by a smaller one at the western end, Ke'e (avoidance). The lagoons provide abundant seaweed, shrimp, octopus, and many kinds of fish. Ha'ena is crowned by the peak Makana (gift) that rises above Ke'e lagoon.

Tunnels

Makua Beach, called Tunnels, is a major attraction for locals and visitors alike. It has appeared in many movies, including *Pagan Love Song* (1950), *Body Heat* (1981), and *Soul Surfer* (2011). Tunnels is also where Buzzy falls in love with his dolphin in the Tiki Goddess mystery novels by Jill Marie Landis. (HCR itself plays a role as the "Ha'ena Beach Resort" in the Tiki Goddess mystery novel *Three to Get Lei'd.*) Notably, Makua provides a famous surf break. Dick Moody came to Kaua'i just to surf it:

> Mom would stay inside the surf line and just bob, and I'd ride my surfboard. Surfing was great. Not in front of our place, down at Tunnels. You had to go to Tunnels to surf. And to snorkel, and let Mom bob around because you couldn't do it in front of our places. I found out about Tunnels from my friends who were from here and told me about the great surfing and great snorkeling, and encouraged me to come on over.

Dick first came here in the 1960s and thus may be considered a surf pioneer.

Boat trips to Na Pali are common nowadays. They leave from the Hanalei River mouth or from Port Allen Harbor on the south side. But when the boats first started taking passengers on trips to the Na Pali coast, the Captain Zodiac tour boat launched from Tunnels Beach. Chuck Williams remembers those trips:

> That's where you actually got into the zodiacs, at Tunnels Beach. And then we went out onto the Na Pali coast. And we went into the caves. And that was just so…gratifying. Because everybody got nice and wet, you just wore your bathing suits.

But not everyone at Tunnels wears a bathing suit. Molly Ksander recalls watching naked visitors. "Guys strut up and down the beach," she says, perhaps with some sarcasm. Some, but not all, of the nudity can be attributed to the Taylor Campers, whom we will meet shortly.

As its fame has spread through the years, the number of visitors drawn to Tunnels has also increased. And so has the problem of parking. Rich Sells saw this as an opportunity: "You used to be able to just park on the road somewhere. You could park anywhere on the road. I almost bought that piece of land right next to the entrance to Tunnels. I was going to turn it into a parking lot and charge five dollars a head."

"But," Nancee pointed out, "there were some restrictions. You couldn't." This is still true. In 2012, local residents tried to do exactly what Sells proposed, although with an up-to-date price. The added parking was very popular, but the authorities terminated the service because it was in a controlled conservation district.

There is little seasonal weather change along the north shore—a slight variation in temperature and the rain pattern, but nothing dramatic, at least for most of the year. The exception is winter storms, which are more intense and more frequent than in other seasons. Tunnels Beach can change drastically when winter storms arrive. Lionel Medeiros describes how Tunnels can change from summer to winter: "When we went to Tunnels in the summertime, it'd be all beach and then you'd go snorkeling. If you'd come in the wintertime—January, February—it's like somebody got a giant knife and cut through the beach and sent all the sand out to the ocean."

Ha'ena | 33

Ha'ena Beach County Park in fair and stormy weather. (From the author's collection)

Tunnels is Bob Johnstone's favorite beach, especially when he's joined by one of the friendly neighborhood dogs that roam the sand:

> Sitting under a tree at Tunnels reading a book and having a sandwich and a couple of beers, and hoping a dog comes by and sits on my lap. Well, I think Ike was my favorite character. Just because he was so cool and he could spend the whole day with me. I'd walk down the beach and people would say, "You sure have a nice dog." To come over and be able to have a dog to spend the whole day with me, it's pretty special.

Marion Burns recalls a funny story about Tunnels, but she says, "I suppose as a grandma, I should not have thought it funny." She recalls a day at Tunnels with her granddaughter:

> She was snorkeling with her father, and she was feeding the fish. One fish bit her enough so that blood was coming out of her finger. And she started to scream as only a ten-year-old or twelve-year-old could scream. She was out there in the water holding up her finger and screaming, "The fish bit me. It bit me!" I thought it was funny.

Her granddaughter, however, probably wouldn't agree.

Legends of the Caves

Ha'ena, too, has its legends. It is noted for its three caves: one dry and two wet. These are the remnants of three lava tubes that were formed when lava flowing from the central volcano cooled and solidified as it moved down to the sea, leaving the caves behind. Local legend gives us insights into understanding the origin of the landscape. The story is that Pele created the three caves when she was searching for a home for herself. When she found only water or dry sand instead of fire, she was not satisfied and so moved on, eventually settling on the Big Island in the active volcano Kilauea, where she found plenty of fire. She dwells there to this day. The tortuous, multi-island love saga of the Ha'ena chief Lohi'au and Hi'iaka, Pele's younger sister, ends at Ke'e Beach, where the lovers reunited and lived happily ever after. The remains of Lohi'au's house are there and have been recognized as an official archeological site. Ha'ena has long been known as a location to search for love and happiness—and retirement.

It is said that the Menehune lived and farmed throughout Ha'ena, and that they took their final departure from Kaua'i in canoes launched from the beach in front of the dry cave Maniniholo. One story claims that the cave itself was created when a local fisherman named Maniniholo dug into the cliff to get rid of "imps" who were sneaking out of the cliff's fissures at night to steal the fisherman's food. Sound suspicious? Maybe not. One evening, after dark, I took a walk past Maniniholo Cave. I was wandering along the cliff face when something above me attracted my attention. I stared for a minute or two and then quickly turned and ran for home, scared to death as never before. Scared of what, I do not know. An imp, perhaps?

The beach in front of the dry cave is Ha'ena Beach Park. It is not protected by a reef, so the surf can be dangerous. Manoa Stream drains across the beach and can also flood. Nevertheless, the beach is locally popular and is a favorite camping ground for many people. Georgia Henry recalls that she would hang out there "with my local friends, listening while they played Hawaiian music. It was a lovely place to be." So it is not all scary. Molly Ksander finds the contrast attractive:

> You can get overwhelmed with the waves and the curve of the bay. It's like the whole ocean's coming at you. Going into the ocean there is kind of scary because you just really feel the power of this great imploding ocean coming at you. On the other hand, you can sit and watch everyone surfing out at Cannons, and it's a very pleasant place.

Archeology, Legend, and History

Archeological evidence suggests that Ha'ena has been settled since around AD 1000. Remains of taro ponds, irrigation canals, dwellings, and heiaus (places of worship) line the valleys all along Manoa and Limahuli Streams. Taro was grown along Manoa and Limahuli Streams, and sweet potatoes were grown on the low flats behind the shore dunes. Dwelling and burial sites have been discovered all along the shore of Ha'ena. Today, we can see how these terraces and irrigation ditches looked if we visit the reconstructed sites in the National Tropical Botanical Garden (NTBG) in Limahuli Valley. Flatland taro fields are also being restored in Ha'ena State Park.

Lava-rock terraces for growing taro in Limahuli Valley. (From the author's collection)

Ke'e was a prominent ancient site of cultural study. Remains of ancient stone structures, including a heiau and hula platform, can still be seen. There was a famous hula *halau*, or school, called *Ka Ulu o Laka* (Inspiration of Laka), where students learned to dance the hula. It was dedicated to Laka, the goddess of hula. It is said that fifty generations of students studied here. One interpretation of the word *Ke'e* is that it was the name of a hula master. The course of study was strenuous and lasted seven years. Many kapus (taboos) had to be observed. One such kapu is captured in a legend. Flowers of the naupaka plant that hedge HCR and many beaches appear to be incomplete because the rays of the flowers only occupy about half of the corolla. A mountain strain of naupaka also exists, and it too is similarly incomplete. Local legend on the north shore tells us that this occurred when two hula students at Ke'e fell in love, thus breaking an important kapu, and appealed to Laka for release from their obligations. The two disappeared, but soon new flowers were seen in the mountains and by the sea, each incomplete by itself but together complete. It was realized that Laka had released the lovers and united them as plants. The final exam required swimming through the lagoon, which contained a large shark. People traveled from all over to attend the hula celebrations at Ke'e.

Ke'e Beach, 1930s. Vegetation is mostly low scrub with only a few isolated trees. (Courtesy Kaua'i Historical Society)

Ke'e was also the location of a school called *Ka Ulu o Paoa* (Inspiration of Paoa), where students studied history and genealogy. These were communicated through chanting, allowing students to learn this vocal art as well. Graduation required that the student listen to a genealogy chant that was several hours long and then repeat it with no errors. Paoa was a *kahuna nui* (high priest and councilor) and a friend of the Ali'i Lohi'au. As such, he played a dramatic role in the story of Pele on Kaua'i. This performance tradition continues to the present day in Ha'ena, which has been home to a number of prominent nineteenth- and twentieth-century chanters, as well as contemporary singers, songwriters, and dancers. These include many of the artists who perform at HCR and the Mediterranean Gourmet.

Moreen Williams:

> When you're at Ke'e, if you go up the path to the hula grounds—it's sacred, so you've got to be very respectful of it—it's beautiful up there. It's a gorgeous view of Ke'e Beach and out into the ocean. You just don't realize the different perspective that you get from up there versus just looking at the beach while you're on the beach.

Makana Peak was made famous as the edenesque Bali Hai in the movie *South Pacific* (1958). Makana (gift) was long the site of a famous fire-throwing ritual, the *'oahi* (fireworks). Skilled climbers would carry hala and hau (sea hibiscus tree) branches up to the peak. Here they would light the sticks on fire and toss them high into the night air, where the updrafts from the mountains would carry them flying out to sea. Prizes were awarded to the best fire stick thrower. In 1913, the *Garden Island* described how the breeze "made the floating sticks of fire seem possessed with life, like so many immense fireflies at gambol in the air." People from all over the island were present for the annual celebration and declared it "the best in many years." A local resident told C. Andrade that the fire throwing was last performed in 1928.

The Land: From Communal to Personal

Through the early 1800s, Ha'ena was organized as a traditional *ahupua'a* based on mutual sharing of common resources throughout the locality. Today it consists of many separate, privately owned properties. How did it change from the one to the other? As with Wainiha, the process started with the *Mahele*. Abner Paki was granted the *ahupua'a* of Ha'ena in the *Mahele*. This was Royal Patent 3596. Abner Paki was from a line of high chiefs on Maui. He was a close friend of King Kamehameha III and served several roles in the king's government. He was also the *hanai* (adopted) father of Queen Liliuokalani. Paki appointed a woman, E. Kekela, to be konohiki, or manager, of Ha'ena. Kekela was related by marriage to both Kamehameha I and Kaumuali'i, the high chief of Kaua'i. Paki married the king's niece, Laura Konia, and they had a daughter named Bernice Pauahi Bishop, who inherited Ha'ena when Paki died in 1855. In her will, Mrs. Bishop created the Bishop Estate, which supports the Kamehameha Schools for Hawaiian children. The estate consists principally of Mrs. Bishop's lands throughout the Islands. In our area, for example, Lumaha'i Valley is part of the estate; however, Ha'ena did not become part of the Bishop Estate. Rather, W. H. Pease, an early surveyor, bought the *ahupua'a* for $1,200 in 1866. In 1872, William Kinney bought Ha'ena from the Pease estate for $1,200—no real estate bubble there.

In the *Mahele*, roughly two dozen smaller plots of land (*kuleana*) within the Ha'ena *ahupua'a* were awarded to individuals who could show that they lived and farmed there. Such plots included house lots, taro ponds, and dry-land plantings and pasture (*kula*). These individual landowners formed the basis of another association of landowners, like that in Wainiha. In 1875, a group consisting of thirty-eight descendants of those awarded *kuleana* in the *Mahele* formed the *Hui Ku'ai Aina o Ha'ena*, or Organization to Purchase Land in Ha'ena. The group's goal was to purchase the entire *ahupua'a* from Kinney. (Carlos Andrade, in his book *Ha'ena: Through the Eyes of the Ancestors*, has told the story of the hui in informative and entertaining detail.) The total cost was $1,500. This association of owners then held Ha'ena in common until 1965. The Ha'ena Hui was organized like the Wainiha Hui—much like a condominium owners' association would be organized today. The officers included a manager, treasurer, and secretary, all with the duties we would expect of similar officers today. A set of bylaws governed the responsibilities and interactions of the members. The hui met in a location called the Ha'ena Hall. Some special considerations accommodated the local conditions. For example, the bylaws stated that each share of hui land entitled members to roam ten animals each. By 1922, this had increased to twenty animals. In addition to his *kuleana*, one share entitled a member to select two and a half acres of *kula* land and two and a half acres of wetland for personal use. The manager had to be consulted on the selection, and the board had to approve. "Notable Places," such as the dry cave, the two wet caves, Makana, and the heiau at Ke'e, were set aside as places for the public to visit. The bylaws also stated that the manager was personally privileged to have, among other things, firewood and specific *he'e* (octopus) hunting grounds along the shore. At the HCR homeowners' meeting in 2011, the board presented the general manager, Laura Richards, with a bundle of firewood to symbolize our historical continuity with Ha'ena of old. The board made no provision at that time for octopus hunting.

Announcement in the *Polynesian* (July 16, 1853) of Land Commission award of Ha'ena *ahupua'a* to Abner Paki, whose is the first name listed. (Library of Congress: Chronicling America: Historic Newspapers)

In 1900, the first federal census following the 1893 overthrow of the Hawaiian monarchy by western-oriented businessmen in Honolulu recorded at least seven households in Ha'ena, and the second census in 1910 showed fifteen households. Historical records show that there was a small community at Ha'ena with a school and a church. In 1917, the school was moved from Ha'ena to Wainiha at the "flat just beyond the Wainiha Valley." The hui provided a lot located close to where HCR is today, on the road across from the beach just east of HCR toward Wainiha Stream. The site is currently undeveloped. The move was intended to provide more convenient access for the students and teachers, because this was where "most of the children" were, according to the *Garden Island*. By 1945, the Ha'ena Church had joined with the Wai'oli Church and Anini Church to form the Wai'oli Hui'ia Church, which met (and still meets) in Hanalei. The Wai'oli Hui'ia Church owned one share of the Ha'ena Hui. The *Honolulu Star-Bulletin* reported a year-round population of sixty people in 1946 and a total of twenty-nine homes in 1957. Mary McGregor often visited Ha'ena a few years later and remembers that "there were little roads where the Hawaiians had these little houses. They would have a turtle shell around the door because there were so many turtles, and a lot of the houses had grass growing on the roof." In the early 1980s, there was a proposal to create a volunteer fire department at Ha'ena, with a truck located near the YMCA Camp and with HCR serving as the location for a twenty-four-hour alarm telephone, but this was not realized. The 2010 federal census recorded 431 residents in Ha'ena. This increase reflects the observations of many people that the greatest change they have seen in Ha'ena is the growth in the number of dwellings.

There were paniolo in Ha'ena. (Paniolo are cowboys, named after the language of the Mexicans—*Españoles*—who first taught Hawaiians about cattle ranching in the mid-1800s.) Cattle and horses were grazed on the flatlands along the shore and lower levels of the valleys. Limahuli Valley was a cattle ranch. Travel back and forth in the service of ranching was common. People talk about cows and horses wandering loose in Ha'ena, even as late as the 1960s. In fact, cattle grazing occurred throughout the valleys of Na

Pali. Cissie Meyer recalls that stray cattle were numerous in Kalalau Valley when she was there in the 1970s. Cattle were brought east to market along what is now the Kalalau Trail. According to Carlos Andrade's book, *Ha'ena: Through the Eyes of the Ancestors*, one resident preferred to ride a cow along the trail rather than a horse because it was more surefooted.

Cattle grazing in Ha'ena. The peak Makana is in the background. (Courtesy Kaua'i Historical Society)

Cattle were taken to Wainiha, where they were driven into the water to swim out to waiting ships or were loaded into boats from a pier at the beach. After a railroad was constructed north to Kilauea, the cattle were also driven there to be boarded on trains. A well-established system for transporting cattle east toward Wainiha for sale and for returning supplies west, back to Ha'ena, was in use. Well-trained horses were often used to transport supplies without riders. Mules were also used by the Wainiha General Store to deliver supplies to Kalalau Valley. Oftentimes, HCR folk, sometimes by themselves and sometimes in groups of three or four, will take a leisurely stroll along the nearby roads that run past those onetime grazing lands. They report that cattle are still grazing.

Rider on road in Wainiha, 1915, possibly on the bank of the Wainiha River as the road goes inland to the bridge crossing. (From the J. Senda Studio. Courtesy Kaua'i Museum)

The Ha'ena Hui continued to own and operate Ha'ena cooperatively until the second half of the twentieth century. Cultivation of taro and other crops in Ha'ena also continued under the hui. In 1881, a company of taro planters called Mahuiki and Company is said to have owned nine hundred acres.

Shares in the hui were passed on to descendants, sometimes becoming more and more divided over time, and shares were also bought and sold throughout this period, so that many people whose families had not been part of the original hui and did not live in the *ahupua'a* now came to own shares. Many people were members of both the Wainiha Hui and the Ha'ena Hui. In fact, there was more than one instance in which the same person was president of both organizations—James K. Apolo and William H. Rice are two examples. Due to the fractionation of shares and lack of heirs in some families, problems arose in administering the affairs of the hui. In 1955, two members of the hui, John Gregg Allerton (also known as John W. Gregg) and Paul G. Rice, instituted legal action to dissolve the hui and redistribute the land. The court created a commission (made up of H. C. Wedemeyer, Y. Yamaura, and N. Akana) to manage the dissolution in a fair and just way for all concerned. The process was extremely complicated. It lasted more than a decade and was completed in 1967. The commission's division of the land is the basis for the current property boundaries in Ha'ena. Several culturally important parcels were assigned to the county, including the wet and dry caves and the sites of the heiau, hula school, and Lohi'au's house at Ke'e. The local county water supply also derives from the partition. The general public benefited through the maintenance of passageways to the cultural sites and the eventual creation of Ha'ena State Park.

Taylor Camp

A particularly interesting event—a phenomenon, really—occurred on the path to the state park. This event was typical of its time, the 1960s, and resonates still within the HCR community. In the late 1960s, Howard Taylor, who was the brother of actress Elizabeth Taylor, purchased a parcel of oceanfront land just west of Limahuli Stream. He wanted to build a house there (some gossip says it was actually a hotel), but this project never came to fruition because the state planned to turn the area into a state park. (This eventually happened, and the area is now known as Ha'ena State Park.) In 1969, however, Taylor allowed several young surfers and counterculture folk to live rent-free on his property. Their numbers soon increased, and they improvised increasingly sophisticated dwellings and support structures, including the tree houses for which they became famous. Tree houses were favored, since they allowed high surf and storm surge to roll up under the structures without damaging them. (Interestingly, modern construction codes require that houses along the shore must be built upon stilts to achieve the same effect as the tree houses.) Some of the dwellings were built from found materials—such as discarded windows and doors from demolished plantation camp buildings, and other recycled materials—and all were creatively customized. This settlement became known as Taylor Camp. The term *camp* was apparently used in analogy to the village-like living accommodations that had been provided for workers during the plantation days. Nancee Sells reports that Taylor Camp "was very ingenious; these people were very creative in what they did to put together this community." The campers developed their own public water and waste systems. The camp had its own rules and internal managers, and it had a softball team that was sponsored by Hanalei Liquor Store and was active in the interisland league. They also formed a band that played in various locations around the island. *Commune* is an imprecise term—Taylor Camp appears to have been more of a community of like-minded people and less of a commune with a single ideology or vision. Unexpectedly, perhaps, Taylor Camp crossed paths with HCR at several points.

Coincidentally, the year that Taylor Camp was founded, 1969, was also the year that HCR was completed. Several members of Howard Taylor's family worked at HCR at one time or another. Howard Taylor's wife, Mara, worked in the HCR office and had a striking feature much like her famous sister-in-law: "Those gorgeous eyes!" remembers Claire Walker. Howard's daughter, Jane, also worked in the office. "Jane was a very pleasant person and used to smile when people would come in and complain," remembers Howard Koch. "Yeah. Beautiful girl," agrees Janne Hayward. The Taylor ladies were not the only good-looking people in the family. Nancee Sells remembers that Howard himself had "the most gorgeous violet eyes I have ever seen. He was drop-dead gorgeous!"

Howard's son, Tommy, also worked at HCR. He became a gardener and made several significant contributions to the HCR landscape. He built our original barbecue and created the plantings at the entrance to the parking lot and in the area framed by the E, F, G, and H buildings.

The campers could often be seen around HCR. They would visit the bar at the Anchorage for dancing. Then, too, the presence of the Taylor Campers was sometimes hard to miss around HCR itself for a very particular reason. Claire Walker recalls "the stories about walking out here and seeing people totally nude, wearing a mask and flippers, wading out into the water without any clothes on." Mary McGregor laughs as she remembers, "Auntie Louise and I would fish along here, and here they come, and no clothes—the guys, you know." The local police would often drop by to visit with Mary. "They would come in the morning, and there'd be pineapples left on the lanai. They would stop for coffee, and we'd report about the hippies, what's going on. We'd find out what the hippies were doing." When the campers had difficulties with the state, Legal Aid provided them with a local attorney, Max Graham, to make sure their rights were protected. A little later, HCR itself benefited from Graham's legal skills, notably in the parking lot conflict with Charo's Restaurant.

Taylor Camp also held a certain attraction for some members of the HCR community. The stories of Taylor Camp remind my wife, Molly, and me of the time when we lived in Drop City, a geodesic dome community in southern Colorado, in the late 1960s. "If it was the 1970s, I would have been down the road; I wouldn't have been here," laughs Molly. Future HCR owner John Brekke, just finishing high school, worked summers on a banana farm above Wailua and would often hang out at Taylor Camp. He especially remembers the sunset celebrations: "And then, at sunset—somebody there had a generator—they would put out these big speakers and start playing the Dead and Creedence and Hendrix and Quicksilver and Jefferson Airplane, and people were dancing on the beach. There was a lot of fun and joy about that."

Moreen and Chuck Williams were also drawn to Taylor Camp. Moreen recalls:

> The first time we came here, we went down to Taylor Camp. We were only twenty-four at the time. We were laughing because there were all these guys out there in tents. Taylor Camp had just started getting set up, because this was in '69. We were laughing because we were seeing that there were all these guys trying to drop out so they wouldn't get drafted for the war. They were thinking in terms of "this isn't even the United States," which, obviously, it was. They weren't living in the trees yet. They had tents made out of tarps. It was very primitive, but they were very happy. I said to Chuck, "This looks really good. You know, we could do this."

Although the local residents had concerns about some aspects of the alternative lifestyle of the campers, such as nudity and drug use, they also shared some interests with the Taylor Campers. The campers' children attended the local school. Cissie Meyer says, "Some of the Taylor Campers became schoolteachers in the area. Some of them were very well liked, and their children went to Hanalei School with the rest of the community. So it was very integrated into the north shore lifestyle."

North shore residents often provided tools, such as backhoes, and taught campers local skills, such as working bamboo. Many campers worked for local farmers. Some neighbors contributed sanitary facilities, and the county picked up the trash. Above all, both residents and campers loved the natural beauty of the area. Campers were famous for swimming to Kalalau Valley and even to Polihale. And they surfed.

In 1977, the state began development of Ha'ena State Park and relocated the remaining campers. Nancee Sells remembers being there when it happened:

> We actually went to Taylor Camp as it was being dismantled. We were there within the last few days, when the authorities had come in and were taking it all apart. That was quite an event to be there when it was actually

being dismantled. There was a little girl—she couldn't have been more than sixteen, maybe fifteen. She was very thin, and she was lying with her head on a log, studying this blade of grass, turning it. We almost stepped on her because we didn't see her right away. She was so out of it; she didn't know whether we were there or not there.

Many former campers are still part of the north shore community. It is now almost impossible to find remnants of the camp within the state park, but John Wehrheim has produced a very enjoyable book and film that document the look and spirit of Taylor Camp. A wonderful novel by John Wythe White, *A High and Beautiful Wave*, tells about a California college teacher who had lived at Taylor Camp in the 1970s and had tried to revisit it in 2001. HCR gets a passing mention in this story.

Taylor Camp may seem to be an anomaly when compared to most other communities. But this way of looking it at may be too limited. We have already seen several styles of communal living on the north shore of Kaua'i. Traditionally, there was the *ahupua'a* system. Then there were the Wainiha and Ha'ena Huis. There is the Association of Apartment Owners, or AOAO, made up of owners of HCR. Taylor Camp was simply another way that people found to satisfy the need for the common resources and organization that we all depend on and enjoy and to balance individual privacy and creativity with social needs. Molly Ksander muses, "Another place, another time, it's almost one and the same. They're both interlocked communities that work by consensus decision-making. HCR is just a more organized commune with a little more money—and flush toilets."

Limahuli Garden

Another result of the dissolution of the Ha'ena Hui was the creation of Limahuli Garden and Preserve. In the partition of the Ha'ena Hui's land, Juliet Rice Wichman received what had been the *ahupua'a* of Limahuli Valley. She stopped cattle ranching there, began to restore the historical taro ponds and canals, and planted native plants. In 1976, she donated the lower portion of the valley to the National Tropical Botanical Garden (NTBG). Her grandson Chipper Wichman further developed the garden and surveyed the upper valley. In 1994, he donated the remaining land in the valley to the NTBG. Carlos Andrade has written and recorded a wonderful song about the valley, also called "Limahuli." Limahuli Garden and Preserve continues to restore its ancient structures and the natural ecosystem using the ancient *ahupua'a* system as a model. According to the Garden's website, "the result is that past and present converge in this lovely valley."

Limahuli Garden provides Molly Ksander with historical insight: "It really gives you the feeling of the whole *ahupua'a* without being a reconstruction. You really get a feeling for the land and the way it changes. You really understand how all those ridges and valleys were made into different communities." Moreen Williams appreciates the view from the garden: "You go up there and you walk around and you keep climbing up; it's probably one of the most spectacular views overlooking the ocean out there." Marion Burns especially likes that "Limahuli is just plants from Kaua'i. Indigenous plants of Kaua'i, which is most interesting." Pat Montague recalls being with her sister up on the hill at the garden and watching whales out to sea.

HCR maintains an intimate relationship with the valley through its offering of a vacation package that includes the opportunity to assist the garden in carrying out its preservation and restoration mission through volunteer work and participation in other garden activities. I first learned about the *ahupua'a* system from a poster in the visitor's center of the garden, so, in a sense, this book has grown from a seed planted in Limahuli Garden.

Ke'e Beach

People often refer to Ke'e Beach simply as "the end of the road." They imply much more than just the termination of an ordinary county road. They often mean the beginning of a place of light and magic, a place of peace and fun. Ke'e is a "very special environment," says Linda Stoskopf, thanks to "the ocean, the lush foliage." The beauty of Ke'e has been celebrated musically in a slack key guitar piece called, appropriately, "Slack Ke'e," by Norman Ka'awa Solomon.

The kamani leaves glistening in the sun on the cliffs above and the dramatic gnarled roots of the ironwood trees on the sand dunes behind the beach figure prominently in the memories of those visiting the beach for the first time and have often been captured in paint by local artists. The gnarled roots continue to be memorable for HCR owners too. Nancee Sells has said, "We go down to the end of the road, you know, where the big tree with the roots that come down. We try to get a picture of anybody that's here with us. We've been doing it for years." Nancee recalls that "they filmed part of *The Thorn Birds* down there. The little green house you used to be able to see from the beach. You could walk up by it; there's that little path that goes up there. But it's overgrown. You can't see it now." This belonged to John Gregg Allerton and was destroyed in the early 1990s.

Memorable roots of ironwood trees at Ke'e Beach. (From the author's collection)

Ke'e exerts a powerful attraction for the HCR community. It is the setting for many vivid memories that trace the course of the day and the passing of the year. Carl Woodbury and his family go early to Ke'e:

> We go really early in the morning before anyone gets there. A lot of times, Jody and I are the only people in the water. It's just absolutely stunning as the sun comes up and looking up at that cliff just standing in that water! It's an unbelievable—it's a mystical experience, no doubt!

Sunset at Ke'e has long been a gathering time. Nancee Sells recalls, "Oh, we'd go down sometimes at 4:00 p.m. We had a little hibachi that we would take. We'd do hot dogs and take the kids. We'd go at four until the sun set, and we'd be in the water. Then, we'd cook our little dinner and watch the sun set." Moreen and Chuck Williams also take sunset at Ke'e seriously. Moreen recalls:

> You go down to Ke'e and you go to the right about a hundred yards and you sit down on the beach and you can see the Na Pali coast and the sunset in the water. I mean, Chuck keeps kidding me because every year we have picture after picture after picture of the same view. "Oh, this year's going to be better." We get green flashes once in a while.

What better place for this elusive experience? And to have it more than once?

Ke'e Beach is, of course, famous as the beginning and end of the Kalalau Trail. Early on, that had an impact on HCR. Dick Moody recalls, "We had the trail—which is world famous, and it was famous then. And the hikers were the only people staying at our colony. When they came off the trail, they had to have a place to sleep and rest up, and so they were the primary tenants of our units."

The sights on the trail were apparently not limited to mountain and sea. Rich Sells recalls, "I remember we used to walk the trail, and the hippies would be totally nude with walking shoes on." Chuck Williams describes a similar experience he and Moreen shared: "On one of the first hikes we took on the Na Pali coast, when we got down to the beach area, there were some fellows running around, and they didn't have a stitch of clothing on at all. It was pretty normal back then."

HCR experiences confirm that caution is needed on the trail. Linda Stoskopf tells of the day their twins, who were teenagers at the time, wanted to hike the trail on a day when Linda and Darrel were not really up for it. So they dropped the kids off at the end of the road.

> We did not tell them to go to the top. We just said, "Watch the time." When we met at the agreed upon time, the kids were exhausted and angry with us because we had allowed them to go on the trail without any water. They still talk about it, and they are thirty-nine. We did not anticipate that they would go so far.

A friend of the Rich Sells, Charlie, actually fell off the trail. Rich remembers:

> We had a group here again for New Year's. [Charlie] was quite a hill climber and had pretty good stamina. They were coming back down. Fortunately, he had this younger fellow with him. His foot just kind of flew out from under. "He did a complete back flip," they said, "went over the edge," and landed on a ledge below the initial trail. Hurt his back, but they were able to get him up and he walked out on his own. But boy, he was in bed the rest of the time, and he didn't go to the doctor while he was here. He's never walked the trail again.

One of Dennie Stansell's fondest memories of Kaua'i occurred at Ke'e Beach:

> Our son and I were out swimming, and the monk seal came up behind me and put his head on top of my head. I must've looked like momma seal out there with the rubber thing on. Our son was out there standing, and this monk seal came right up and looked him in the face.

Moreen Williams also recalls a time when she was at Ke'e with her daughter, swimming:

> [We were] outside of the reef where it's like a shelf. From only three feet deep, it drops down to fifteen or eighteen feet deep. It's almost like a wall. All of a sudden, my older daughter and myself, we were just among five or six giant sea turtles swimming. It was a real kick.

Owen Paepke and his father, Bruce, had some exciting moments swimming at Ke'e. They had "stories that my mother Marion would not have liked to have heard. Perhaps we occasionally overestimated our fortitude out there," says Owen. "If you get on the wrong side of the reef and you go through the channel and are trying to get back in against the tide—that is a whole different fish." On the less risky side, they also enjoyed rinsing off in the cold pool in the Limahuli Stream.

Carl Woodbury had his own scary moment at Ke'e. He was swimming in the lagoon and accidentally got outside the reef while the tide was going out. "Getting back in through that channel was a bit of a swim. But other than that, not a big deal. You do have to pay attention to the ocean here, because the water does move."

Ke'e changes dramatically with the seasons. Lionel Medeiros illustrates this:

> We usually like to snorkel on the left side of the beach and up toward the mountains because that'd be like

> twelve feet of water. But yeah, we've gone out there with the sand shifted so much that we'd literally walk out to the reef. You try to explain that to people and they say, "No way."

Molly Ksander also appreciates the contrasts offered by Ke'e in the winter, "when the wild waves come crashing across the rocks," she says.

> That's where you see the waves that look like horses galloping. They're just overwhelming. Then at other times, it's almost a peaceful pond—for snorkeling and just wandering along the edges. It's just a little special place that holds you. And the trees. And wandering in the trees.

Ke'e Beach has served as a location for several movies, among them *Pagan Love Song* (1950), *The Thorn Birds* (1983), *Lord of the Flies* (1990), *Throw Momma from the Train* (1987), and *Pirates of the Caribbean: On Stranger Tides* (2011). HCR folk often watch these just for the fun of identifying familiar local landmarks. Most famously, *South Pacific* (1958) was filmed throughout Ha'ena, and Makana Peak played a starring role. It is fitting, therefore, that the HCR community pay tribute to the film. Moreen and Chuck Williams and their children have dramatically contributed to this effort, as Moreen describes:

> This is from the very beginning of us bringing our kids down here because of the movie *South Pacific*. We've sat out here on the beach, and then again, at Tunnels Beach. And we've done it at Ke'e. Sang the whole score of *South Pacific*. My kids know the whole score. I know the score. We've sung all the way up the shore.

What a tribute indeed!

Aggie Parlee used to walk along the beach from HCR to Tunnels and back, and now her grandson does the same. Marion Burns would walk from HCR to Ke'e and back. Barbara and Bob Johnstone sometimes spend a day going to Ke'e. They walk from HCR to Ke'e to have lunch, and then they walk back to HCR, entirely along the beach. Bob Eckert also walks from HCR to Ke'e and back, but he prefers to travel out by the shore and return by road "to take advantage of the winds." This is a great opportunity to meet all of the local friends he has known for years. Whether coming or going, these walkers really get the best of all worlds—Wainiha and Ha'ena by land and sea!

Chapter 5

Talk Story—What It Is

It is almost sundown. Several couples meet accidentally when they come down to barbecue their fish and ribs and vegetables on the old grill on the edge of the central courtyard. Perhaps there is some wine from an old vine. They sit and watch the line of evening clouds form familiar shapes as they parade in from the bluffs of Princeville: birds in flight, Snoopy on a skateboard, ice cream cones, distant kingdoms. One of the couples bought their apartment only two weeks ago, so this is their first opportunity to meet and chat with other owners. They are very new to the property and have many questions. As they meet new people, they repeatedly gush, "Oh, we love this place! But what is it? What does it mean to you? Why are you here?" The longtime owners grin and reply.

HCR is many things. It is a business, a historical connection, a vacation spot, an investment, a residential community, and a hotel.

HCR is home for some and a home away from home for many; it is a retreat, a hideaway, and a healing spot. It is a place to live and a way of living. "It's all those things. It really can be what you want it to be. Whether you want the social and the interactive, the adventuresome and the physical, or the simple solitude of not talking to anyone for two weeks, you can," muses Molly Ksander.

Home

"No place is like this. You know, where the temperature is pretty even, and the air is so soft, and the trade winds. It's just totally different. Step off the plane and you think, *Oh, I'm back home*," says Claire Walker.

Bob Johnstone feels very much at home at HCR and the north shore: "I can be gone for three months and when I walk in the door, it's like I've just been to the store or something. I go in a restaurant and they call me by name." Cissie Meyer has found that owners look on HCR "in that same true vein of really loving the property and caring about Hanalei Colony as a second home, not just a rental property." Aggie Parlee says, "The people that come here, they act like it's part of their home."

"Truly, it is kind of a part-time home," says Darrel Stoskopf, "friendly people, glad to see you; you are glad to see them." For a time, Georgia Henry lived at HCR when she was the manager. "Living there, to this day, it's home to me. I loved it. Its location—the whole ambiance of that place is my fondest memory." Dick Moody puts it simply: "Drive up to it, get the key, and I'm home."

HCR feels like home, and it may sometimes look like home, too. Dennie Stansell talks about her first impression of the place, which is "from when I stopped at the overlook at Princeville." She continues:

> I grew up in the Shenandoah Valley of Virginia. There is a famous overlook near Charlottesville, Virginia. And when I stopped at Princeville, it was like, "Oh my God, that's where I grew up!" Except that they're growing taro instead of corn or wheat. That's the valley; that's a green valley. Then they had these split-rail fences, the zigzaggy fences, around the airport at Princeville. They're not there now. But again, that was like the farmland of rural Virginia. It felt like a homecoming.

Tommy Richards sees that "owners just love coming here because this is home. I think everybody thinks this is home."

This sense of home is partially the result of the fundamental stability of HCR. Although people see slow changes in the details, the overall picture stays the same in their minds. The mountains and the sea are always present. The buildings look the same—their structure, their color. When people go to HCR, they know what to expect. They can relax.

They don't need to worry about surprises, and they can be confident that their familiar surroundings and comforts will be there. It is "a place that is ours to go to; our stuff is there; our corner is there; it is a known; it is a place we love," explains Molly Ksander.

It is not just HCR that provides stability, but the whole north shore. John Brekke senses it in Hanalei: "I love Hanalei town. Hanalei town is just so nice because it just hasn't changed in all the time—forty-five years. I mean, you know, they've painted it up, the stores have changed, and the school is now a restaurant. But basically, it hasn't changed." (Although you rarely see people riding horses through Hanalei these days, as Cissie Meyer remembers seeing in the 1970s.) Moreen Williams recalls: "But the Ching Young Center and all, those pretty much look the same today as they looked in 1969. Then, when we started coming back in 1980–81, so they look pretty much the same. That's what's so nice about it here."

Bob Johnstone also believes that the place has "changed fairly little in the overall scheme." He explains:

> Making this road a historic highway [Highway 560 was listed on the National Register of Historic Places in 2004] was good, and the bridge, of course, it kind of limits things out here. This area has been fairly protected, and that's one of the things we like so much about it.

Aggie Parlee gets right to the heart of the matter: "The ocean's always here, and it's always beautiful."

Not Just an Investment

It is interesting that few people say that they arrived at HCR because they were looking for an investment, although that is often what they received as a side effect, almost in spite of themselves. A former owner from Canada described such an experience in the minutes of the annual meeting of the rental program members in 1999.

> She and her husband wanted to know everything possible about the resort, and pestered Laura Richards for reams of information. After reading all the material sent, she and her husband concluded they would be purchasing property of marginal construction in a hurricane and tsunami area. They decided to purchase because they loved the area and because of the way the property is run. Shortly after they purchased their condominium, their accountant gave his opinion that HCR was one of the most favorable investments he had seen for such out-of-country investments.

Similarly, say Nancee and Rich Sells, "When we started looking at the financials, this place was not making any kind of money at all. If we got a distribution, it was like $200. It was simply a matter of heart over mind." Dick Moody did not expect to make any money off the place, nor does his daughter. It was not the income that initially brought Linda and Darrel Stoskopf to HCR, but they do look at it as a special kind of rental, "a valuable rental property that is available to us on short notice and is truly a retreat, a special retreat." HCR is many things at once.

A Place for Fun

Vacations are for fun. At HCR, fun includes the things you might expect: beach time, snorkeling, hiking, fishing, Tahiti Nui. "Everything I do here is fun," says Bob Johnstone. He goes on:

> I can get up someday and never leave my lanai and have fun. I can be extremely active—we got up at 5:00 a.m., went to Lumaha'i, and found a nice sunrise show. Or I can just sit on the lanai and read books all day and then go down to the barbecue in the evening.

Carl Woodbury and his family also have a lot of fun: "We've had so many good experiences here. The breakfasts are fun, the hikes up on top of the swamp and the top of the mountain are fun. It's kind of like an outdoor, adult Disneyland." Darrel Stoskopf recalls a helicopter trip that landed at the base of a waterfall for a swim and champagne lunch. "It was like leaving this world and going to another one." Tommy Richards suggests that HCR plays an active role in helping folks enjoy the island:

> We give the guest a chance to get out and do—to see the island. We kind of force you to get outside to the beach, or do the hike, walk into Hanakapi'ai up to the falls. We want you to go out and not just stay in your room, to get out and experience the island. That is why you will never see a TV in there.

"I love visiting the place. I love seeing the pretty fish, but when I am here, I am just a tourist and, as an owner, I also recognize some caretaker aspect of it, but the reality is I want to see pretty fish," muses Owen Paepke. For Molly Ksander, fun is "wandering endless back roads. Anywhere, any road, any time. Turn right, turn left. You go makai, and then you follow this down, see where it'll take you. It's always a new adventure. Always a new discovery."

"The most fun, by far, is when the Hawaiians sing—some of them are so good, and they love it," enthuses Mary McGregor.

Fun at HCR also includes time with friends and family: for being with them, watching them grow, and celebrating. Tom Stansell dedicated one trip to getting his eighteen-year-old son scuba certified. He especially recalls a trip with his two grandchildren, who had great fun riding an ATV, pulling in one fish after another, snorkeling, tubing, and taking the Na Pali boat trip. Just being with other HCR folk is fun too. "That was the fun part," reflects Georgia Henry, "people that you really, really enjoyed being with."

A Healing Hideaway

Whatever else it is, for most owners and all guests, HCR is a hideaway. Both may stay for short periods or remain for months at a time.

Both may return frequently or rarely. Oftentimes, guests become owners. However sampled, in big bites or small, HCR provides freedom from daily cares and routines; it provides rest, recreation, recuperation, rehabilitation, and leisure. It allows you to be unplugged or, as Pat Montague says, to get "away to a different place." For Molly Ksander, HCR "has a rhythm of its own, totally separate from your daily life. When you go there, you are cut off from whatever life you leave on the mainland, but you immediately pick up with a rhythm that is uniquely the north shore. And, specifically, HCR." One guest expressed how the rhythm of the sea made this happen for his family, "sitting on the porch and listening to the sounds of the waves crashing, and getting lost in the motion."

For many people, HCR is that magic land, that paradise, to which their minds can travel in any brief moment of immediate need and where their bodies can follow when able. "It's a retreat. It's like a place where you can get inside your own mind. You can find whatever moment or state of mind you need," feels Molly Ksander. Or, as Dick Moody says more colorfully, "My biggest pleasure was just being able, when I'm someplace else, to think, *I can go there*. I mean, I can all of a sudden say, 'Look, I'm going to Kaua'i. I've had enough of this (whatever was happening). I'm going over there.'" HCR is a place for daydreaming—for daydreaming about when you are not there and for just daydreaming when you are.

Molly Ksander believes that HCR provides, as she says, "versions of solitude":

> Whether it's sitting on the beach by yourself, taking a walk alone, or spending hours on the lanai staring at the horizon, you can experience solitude as a state of mind. You get Hawai'i brain from the minute you walk into the property. It's hard to remain focused on business. All the sound you hear is the ocean. All you feel is the trade winds. All you smell is trees and flowers and grass, and sand, and sea. It's a combination that takes your brain and transforms it.

This is also true for Linda Stoskopf, who recalls the "feeling of peace that comes over me when I get off the plane. The stress level just goes down." And for Owen Paepke, "This is, for me, just a sensory experience and a little bit of a break from the world, which we could all use every once in a while. The amazing restorative properties of the tropical biosphere at HCR can sometimes work their magic on people as well." He says that HCR has "man-made isolation," and because of this, "in terms of the developed places in the United States, you cannot really do much better in terms of getting away than how you get away at Hanalei Colony Resort."

Many Kaua'i folks stay at HCR, often for weekend getaways or when visiting family in the area. Lionel Medeiros and Mary Neudorffer live full time on Kaua'i, on the south shore. But even they need a vacation. So they go to the north shore, to HCR, because it is "a healing place. People tend to gravitate more to healing on the island of Kaua'i. And here is another place to come up and heal. Certainly, we love the place, or we wouldn't keep coming back. For us, it's a haven." HCR was able to provide some real healing for Peggy Slater, who was an adventurous sailor, famous as the first woman to sail solo to Hawai'i. She was also a friend of Mary McGregor's. Slater had an accident at sea, and after her rescue, Mary says, "she was really in bad shape." So Mary put her up at HCR to help her recuperate. Linda Stoskopf tells of a "young man from the neighborhood who had had a bad biking accident and had a very challenging time with his mobility. He would use the pool a lot. It was kind of his therapy." These convalescents are not alone.

Part of the lure of HCR as a place to hide away is the sense of completeness it provides, of self-sufficiency, of contentment. Everything you need is here. Some owners are quite content to spend their entire visit locally. "From Hanalei to Ke'e. To me, everything you need, whether it's two days or two months, it's right there," says Bob Johnstone.

Carl Woodbury agrees. "I'm at the point now that we rarely move beyond Kilauea. We just don't leave the north shore anymore." For Linda Stoskopf, day-to-day life at HCR "has definitely changed since our children have grown. We were always on the hunt for body boarding, surf matt riding, hiking. We do not tend to seek those activities out as we did when our children were younger." This may change, however, as the grandchildren come along. "Our six-year-old granddaughter is clamoring to go to HCR, and we are looking forward to introducing her to surfboard riding in Hanalei Bay," says Linda. And other younger grandkids are coming along.

Folks who live nearby are also content. As Debra Jason says, "Most of us who live out this way stay pretty close to home. We love the beauty of the north shore—why go anywhere else?"

Cissie Meyer argues that the convergence of businesses around HCR contributes to this sense of sufficiency:

> The people can stay here on property for days at a time. You've got your day spa, you've got the coffee shop and a little bit of shopping. I mean, it could expand a little bit, a little bit of a sundry shop or something. But it's here—on the property. And then, you've got the bar and the restaurant, computers, and everyone's wireless connection and everything.

Debra Jason sums it up in a few words: "Everything's there, so you never have to leave."

It is quiet at HCR, perhaps with only the murmuring surf or the tweeting of white eyes nesting under the eaves. Lionel Medeiros says,

> You know, the big thing, it was quiet. As soon as they said we have no television, we have no telephones, I thought, *Man, I like this because it's a getaway.* You know, being at work where I had cell phones and pagers and everything else, it's like you can't get away. And here I'm saying, "Man, I don't want anybody calling me up." So I just loved it. Just the getting away.

This search for quiet is a common thread among HCR folk. Before there was an HCR, Mary McGregor would come here to the beach to read, but she did not bring a book. She had a photographic memory, but it did not work if too much extraneous stimulation interfered. "But here I could do it. I could read pages," she says. People in town would say they saw her sitting out on the beach, but she wouldn't remember them because she had been "reading in my head." This is among her fondest memories. "That was the best thing—peaceful, no distraction."

Carl Woodbury says that his oldest daughter, who works in Silicon Valley, and her husband come to HCR "for the same reason that Jody and I bought it, just to not hear any electronics at all, to watch the waves, and to have some good meals. And just completely relax. So it's a family thing for us." The same goes for Marion Burns, who recalls, "From the very beginning, there were no telephones, radios, televisions, so we spent the night playing games." And Linda Stoskopf says, "To me it is very peaceful. I enjoy the tranquility, love being on the water, and having the background noise of the ocean." HCR was, and is, a quiet, unplugged retreat.

The stark contrast between life at HCR and their everyday life may make HCR guests especially sensitive to HCR's healing powers. As one wrote in a guest book:

> The week before leaving, our home was broken into and many valuable things were taken. After spending seven days here, we've grown deeper in our understanding of life. Life is truly what you make of it. With spectacular views of the mountains from the beach and the endless sound of the waves crashing on the beach, how can you not be reminded of the gift that life is? Things can be taken from you, but the memories and experiences of such beauty cannot.

Another guest was also transformed: "I've been a different person—at peace and open to the possibility that life should be simple. Sunrises, sunsets, stars. I will put this place into my center as a source of strength and hope."

"Shhh. Liquid sunshine, rainbows, hissing surf, tropical fish, birds singing—what could be more healing?" asks another.

Does HCR feel like home to you? Is it your retreat? Do you relax here, have fun? Are you daydreaming?

Chapter 6
A Place at the Beach

HCR looks essentially the same today as it did when it was built. The architecture is informal, small, and intimate: two-story wooden frame buildings with gable ends, each containing four units, or apartments, as if four small plantation cottages were bundled together. A lanai for each suite connects the interior and the surrounding natural world. Zigzag wooden exterior stairways and balustraded walkways are a defining feature and are reminiscent of the railed verandahs common on nineteenth-century Hawaiian buildings. The grounds are largely lawn, with planting beds bordering the buildings and the edges of the resort. Sculptural plants, often native, are positioned at strategic spots. The buildings are laid out in an inner rectangle around a grassy courtyard and in outer curved arches along a winding stream. Some buildings stand alone, some are set at right angles, and others are joined at sharp or small angles. The location of three buildings on the opposite side of the stream adds further interest. The orientation and spacing of the buildings provides a variety of small spaces for varied landscaping and gives each little area its own identity within the overall composition. The reception office is in a small one-story wooden cottage at the entrance.

The structures of HCR blend easily into their natural surroundings. The whole resort has a palette of tans and browns and greens. The buildings are the color of the sand and the soil and the walkways. The trim of the buildings and their roofs echo the brown of the earth and the tree trunks. The structures are surrounded below, above, and in between by the green of the lawns and the trees. A red hibiscus, a purple plumeria, and a white spider lily provide contrast. A multicolored whirligig spinning on a lanai announces that the owners are in residence. Altogether, the property is a comfortable and pleasing environment to wander through. It is small enough so that one does not feel overwhelmed by the layout or the size of the structures, and it is varied enough that one is not bored by sameness. The atmosphere is that of a small village. With only a little imagination, it could be a Hawaiian village of old.

Artist's rendering of plan for Ha'i O Kauai Cottage Colony in 1968 promotional brochure. (Courtesy Marion Burns)

Foundations

Sherman Dowsett was a property developer from Honolulu. The Dowsett family has long been an important force in Hawai'i and is still a big name in property development in the Islands, especially on Oahu. In 1966, Dowsett's firm, Ha'ena Development Company, with Theodore R. Di Tullio as president, bought a portion of the Nishimoto property at Kepuhi Point and began to create the project we now know as Hanalei Colony Resort. HCR was built on what had been Lot 77A when the Wainiha Hui was dissolved, and the adjacent restaurant was built on what had been lot 76B. The architect was Donald Chapman, whose Honolulu firm was involved with many significant buildings, including the visitor center at Pearl Harbor in the 1970s and the historic rehabilitation of Waikiki's Moana Hotel (now the Moana Surfrider) in the 1980s. So the design of HCR was in good company. The general contractor was Kenneth Shioi Company, which had a large practice on both Oahu and Kaua'i.

Clearing the scrub brush along the stream, prior to construction of HCR. (Courtesy Mary McGregor)

The property was legally established as a condominium development on December 3, 1968, by a document called the Declaration of Horizontal Property Regime, which defined the structures to be built and the organization and operation of the resulting property. This document has been amended through the years and is still the official governing document of the homeowners' association, officially called the AOAO. A 1968 article in the *Honolulu Star-Bulletin & Advertiser* described plans for the project. The four-acre resort was to include a Polynesian-themed restaurant and, curiously, a motel. The developers planned to have helicopters on call to provide direct transportation from Lihue airport to the "heliport" at the resort. Compact cars would also be available at the airport and the resort. A promotional brochure also described a 180-craft small boat harbor at the nearby Hanalei River.

Construction began in 1967. First, the trees and scrub vegetation that covered the area had to be cleared. Mary McGregor, who frequented the area during the project, described part of the clearing: "Two large mango trees and the mass of hau and plum trees were uprooted. Part of this was already burned. Kamani trees also needed to be rooted out." The waste material was burned, bulldozed, and hauled away to allow room for the foundations to be laid.

HCR under construction. Foundations have been laid. (Courtesy Mary McGregor)

Mary recalls that construction was fast, lasting approximately a year. Units were on sale for $24,650 to $27,900. Maintenance fees were estimated at twenty-eight dollars per month, per unit. The grand opening took place at noon on September 28, 1969, with a "Paniola [sic] Chuckwagon Luncheon," (recalling the area's cowboy history) with the restaurant and motel scheduled to open early the next year. Sales appear to have been brisk. In 1973, prices were in the range of $30,000 to $40,000.

The A building under construction. (Courtesy Mary McGregor)

When development began, the project was called Bali Ha'i Cottage Colony. This was likely a reference to "Bali Ha'i" in the 1958 movie *South Pacific*. Before completion in 1969, the name was changed to Ha'i O Kauai Cottage Colony. The Hawaiian word *Ha'i* has several meanings. One is "edge or border." On Kaua'i it may also mean "house." According to the *Star-Bulletin & Advertiser*, the name of Dowsett's development referred to a "cottage on the beach at Kaua'i" and was described as "one of the most unusual, 'out of the way' resort complexes in the Islands." In 1979, the name of the resort was legally changed again to the current Hanalei Colony Resort to strengthen the association with the Hanalei region for guests. This name had been used informally before that time, as shown by the invitation to the 1969 opening luncheon.

> THE OWNERS OF THE NEW
>
> HANALEI COLONY RESORT
>
> AT HAENA, KAUAI
>
> CORDIALLY INVITE YOU
>
> TO THEIR GRAND OPENING AND A
>
> PANIOLA CHUCKWAGON LUNCHEON
>
> 12 NOON
>
> SEPTEMBER 28, 1969

Invitation to luncheon held to celebrate the grand opening of Hanalei Colony Resort. (Courtesy Marion Burns)

When first developed, the property was probably intended primarily as a residential condominium. It is not clear how the motel was to operate. Although individual owners had the right to lease their units, a formal rental program was not put into place until later, as we shall see. Many of the original owners were based on Oahu, and it is likely that they purchased the property in the hope of being able to resell it for a profit. At first, Dowsett leased the land associated with each condominium to buyers through 1999, a period of thirty years, with the right to renegotiate another twenty-five years until 2024. He and his wife, Carol, retained fee simple ownership of the land. That is, they continued to own the land on which the buildings were erected and leased this to the purchasers, who owned the structure of the buildings. Purchase of buildings through leasehold has long been a very common practice in Hawai'i. This kind of arrangement can be a problem when the lease expires and the original owner does not wish to extend it. The origin of HCR as a leasehold has not been a source of trouble for the later owners, because the leaseholds soon went away. It did, however, lead to one significant problem for HCR. We shall see more of this problem in a moment.

A Place at the Beach | 73

Aerial photo of Ha'i O Kauai Cottage Colony in 1969. The recreation area and swimming pool are not yet built. A few houses can be seen around the resort. (Courtesy HCR Archives)

In 1976, Theodore "Ted" James, who was a real estate broker from Honolulu, bought the fee simple rights to the HCR property from Dowsett's estate, along with a number of unsold units, including the H and I buildings. He also bought the restaurant property, which he sold in 1978. (I will give you a taste of the restaurant story in chapter 8.) James then began to sell the fee simple ownership rights to individual condo lessees and to the homeowners' association. Those who bought the fee simple rights then also owned, in addition to their own apartment and a portion of the common facilities, a share of the entire four acres of land on which the resort was built. Dick Moody thinks he may have been one of the first owners to purchase a unit "when the land was part of the sale."

Thus, unit by unit, the property changed from being owned by a single person, Dowsett or James, to being owned communally by the members of the AOAO. At first, the fee simple rights were priced at about $8,000, but the price soon began to rise. The Walkers paid $8,800, and soon others were paying $11,000. This process raised occasional issues. Claire Walker recalls that when she and her husband purchased their apartment, the previous owners had not paid for the fee simple rights, and this had to be done before they could complete the purchase. James also purchased the entire I building, and all four units were in his wife's name. The AOAO bought unit L-2 around 1973 and bought the fee simple rights for apartment L-2 as well as for the laundry shed and the office building, or cottage, as it was called, in 1979. The last leasehold was converted to fee simple by Rich and Nancee Sells as late as 1998.

Some of the original and very early owners include Jesse and Bunny Alexander, Marion Burns, Gordon Damon, Ted and Mary James, Mary and Dee (Dolores) McGregor, Tom Moffatt, Donald Monroe, Shirley and Patrick Olds, Kathy Scesney, and Ailene Smart. Mary and Dee (until her passing in 2013) later lived full time at HCR. Many of these original owners made significant contributions to the resort and continue to be part of its living history.

Once built, the resort continued to develop. Significant additions to the common areas occurred, and improvements in the layout and amenities of individual units were continuously made. All of these changes greatly enhanced the quality of life for the people of HCR. Let's take a look at some of the major additions to the common areas that have had a material impact on the way of life of the HCR community today.

The Barbecue Area

Over the years, many owners have become lifelong friends with each other and with staff members, especially those who live on site. Many owners and longtime staff happily recall delightful times socializing together and, especially, sharing communal meals and potluck events. The barbecue area near the central courtyard was a very early addition to the resort and may have existed from the very beginning. Howard Koch remembers that Howard Taylor's son, Tommy, a nephew of Elizabeth Taylor, built the original barbecue, and Claire Walker says that her husband, Dusty Walker, took it upon himself in the mid-1980s to tile the structure using material left over from tiling his bathroom. "They did it beautifully, and it's still a very popular spot," says Georgia Henry. This is the same cinder-block barbecue that is used today. The tradition of holding owners' parties began around the barbecue.

Originally, the barbecue pit was not covered by a roof, as it is now. Rich and Nancee Sells and Georgia Henry recall that the diners would sit under a nearby false kamani tree that kept them completely dry. "The kamani tree leaves were very, very large," Georgia says. Sadly, the tree had to be cut down because its roots were interfering with the plumbing. The Sells and Claire Walker recall that the barbecue group put up with wet dinners for a while until the roof was installed. After some delay in constructing the gazebo, Rich Sells forced the issue by threatening to build it himself. In the end, the Maintenance Supervisor, Steve Pastore, built the gazebo around 1995.

The barbecue has long been one of the prime locations for memorable social occasions. Bruce Paepke considered himself something of an artist at the barbecue, and he demonstrated this every night. According to his son, Owen, Bruce would buy fish directly off the boats tied up near what is now the Hanalei Dolphin Fish Market and get tips from the fishermen on preparation: "How long to cook it and should it be medium or medium rare, what marinade you should use, if any—because the answer may well be 'none.'" This set the stage for the inevitable socializing. "He would go out there and he would have some rum—he was the first to share that—and people would stop by and chat with him all the time. I would just kind of soak that in."

"That's how you really get acquainted is out standing around that barbecue," says Claire Walker. This is also true for Bob Johnstone, who says that "for me, the best way to get the other owners and guests together was down at the barbecue at night. Get down there and just kind of mix and mingle, and it's kind of fun down there." Among Janne Hayward's fondest memories is "the people that I've met. You know, you sit around the barbecue and you talk story with people."

The swimming pool is another fabled location that has nurtured unforgettable social events. These spanned the gamut from simple personal Zen moments to ambitious group festivities—and many in between.

Swimming Pool and Recreation Area

When initially completed, the resort did not have a swimming pool. Over time, the owners became increasingly interested in building one. In addition, as Janne Hayward recalls, hospitality experts consulted in support of the rental program strongly suggested that a pool was needed to attract mainland guests. This became especially important when Princeville was completed as a full-service resort. But owners were somewhat divided on the question of where the pool should be built. Some proposed that it be located in the courtyard, the large grassy area in the middle of the buildings. This would be most convenient, and for many there was no other obvious location. Marion Burns recalls, "I thought it would be lovely to have an apartment right there overlooking the pool." But others did not want the peace and quiet and their view of the ocean to be disturbed by activities at the pool. "Can you imagine the pool being there?" asks Aggie Parlee with disapproval.

The question was answered in 1977 when the homeowners' association purchased from Ted James the additional land behind the resort and adjacent to the road. At the time, this was part of the restaurant property and served as a parking lot. Claire Walker and Marion Burns recall that a helicopter would land there from time to time. (Laura Richards remembers that one time the helicopter actually crashed! It was one of the first helicopters on the island, and according to Laura, Red Johnson was the operator. "He was just this crazy guy," she says. In addition to providing tours, Johnson would use the helicopter for personal favors for islanders: such as flying supplies from stores in Hanalei out to Kalalau Valley residents [on Red Hill] and for his own transportation. "He had landing pads in lots of places. I got dropped into places that I would probably never see again." It was on one of his visits to a friend at HCR that the chopper went down.)

Once the new land was purchased, the recreation area was completed in short order. The entire project included a swimming pool, hot tub, guest bathrooms, charcoal barbecues, and a roof (gazebo or pavilion) over the barbecue area. A housekeeping laundry and utility facility were also included. A tennis court had been considered but was not realized. Fritz Johnson, an architect from Honolulu, designed the pool and recreation area. International Pool Company of Kapa'a installed the pool and hot tub, and Russ Boyer's firm from Hanalei did the construction.

Janne Hayward recalls that two second mortgages for $65,000 and $50,000 were obtained to pay for the property and the pool construction. To complete the recreation area, owners performed some of the manual labor and finish work themselves. They planted the hibiscus bushes. "They got a bush of hibiscus and they cut little sticks off of it, and they stuck them in the ground. They all grew up into great big bushes," recalls Marion Burns. Dusty Walker tiled the hot tub area. The pool was finished in 1981. A special assessment of $1,000 per unit was made to complete the final work.

Then there was a fire. It was scary and disruptive. In 1984, a defective florescent light fixture triggered a blaze in the laundry room, not the Wishie Washie Hale (house) used by the owners and guests, but the housekeeping laundry facility. According to Georgia Henry, the manager at the time,

> The fire destroyed every single thing in the laundry room. That was July 31. We were booked full on August 1. I went immediately to Lihue and contracted for all our cleaning supplies, all of our laundry equipment, including a washer and dryer. So that started our business day August 1, and we finished with the biggest August we'd ever had in the history of the resort. It turned out to be something quite wonderful, but the stress of it was not wonderful.

The laundry was soon repaired.

The very existence of the pool triggered some laughs. When Owen Paepke and his father first saw the pool, they laughed mockingly, "God, it is the biggest ocean in the world just steps away and you need a swimming pool!" Nevertheless, they were soon converted. "We kind of caught on to the fact that this could be a nice thing to be able to take a dip in the fresh water after you were in the ocean water and just rinse off the salt, but somehow Dad and I were not bright enough at the beginning to connect that. Our views definitely changed after that."

The location of the pool soon came to be seen as an excellent choice. "It was the biggest relief to me that they did not put the pool in the courtyard," says Aggie Parlee. Nancee Sells was one who had originally wanted the pool located in the lawn area but is now glad that she was outvoted. Marion Burns agrees: "I didn't realize how windy it would have been. So it really is in a fine place now." The new barbecue facility in the recreation area stimulated a little skepticism because it was remote. "How would you see anybody?" asked Bruce Paepke. "They are over in the midst of the buildings, and that is where somebody will come and have a drink and talk about the fish, which is what you want." It quickly became apparent, however, that this would not be a problem. The new recreation area—and its barbecue—soon became the site of notable events and celebrations. Some were humble family occasions. Janne Hayward says, "It was just so fun to go over and cook some fish from the Dolphin at the barbecue area while the kids go swim and stuff like that."

Other events were more boisterous. One evening that stands out for many people began as a lu'au at the pool. One of the guests was the film actor Robert Mitchum. Now, Dusty Walker, one of the owners, was quite a character. Laura Richards recalls that he dressed exclusively in white—white hat, long white shirt, white shorts, and white shoes. He had been in the entertainment business and was familiar with many people in Hollywood. Dusty and Robert were both accomplished raconteurs, and they began trading Hollywood stories. According to Nancee Sells, "He and Dusty were just in their glory. We listened to story after story about everybody from Marilyn Monroe to John Wayne to Katherine Hepburn. Mitchum knew everybody. And he had a story to tell about everybody."

Eventually the party moved from the pool to the Sells' apartment, and around three thirty or four in the morning, Nancee said, "OK, enough is enough. You have to go home. I mean I basically kicked them out."

The pool area was the original location for the Mai Tai Party when Laura Richards initiated the practice in the mid-1990s. These informal parties—where owners, resort guests, and staff mingle to talk story—are one of the most popular features of HCR. The resort supplies mai tais; owners and guests bring pupu (appetizer) plates and conversation. For many people, these parties are among their fondest memories. It is a particularly good occasion to talk with visitors, see what their experience is like, and offer them local information. It is exhilarating to see first-time visitors, their eyes wide with wonder, as they struggle to express their appreciation of the island and our part of it. The excitement and the learning are often mutual. Guests have also recorded these happy experiences in the memory books provided by the owners of the apartments in which they were staying. HCR also offers a continental breakfast at the pool, and owners would sometimes host these events. Averil Koch recalls, "Jane would pick up the stuff from the snack bar and bring it here, and then we'd all put it out. I'd come up, and maybe bring a neighbor or two with me, and they'd come and help me." Community events like these Mai Tai Parties and pool breakfasts have been wonderful pathways for introducing guests into the HCR 'ohana (extended family).

Over time, the pool came to need refurbishing. "It was almost like a Motel 6 pool," said one owner. In 1992, the pool was tiled, and depth markers were added. After renovation of the residential units in 2010, the pool area was also refurbished and upgraded with additional landscaping and stonework, and a koi pond was added to enhance the recreation area grounds. Owners and guests feel it is now better than ever. It continues to be the site of important HCR events: from family parties to lazy afternoons with a book (or, increasingly, an electronic device). And it continues to evolve and become ever more lush and inviting.

Little Things Can Mean a Lot

Usually the loss of a structure on the property would be disturbing, but the disappearance of one particular structure was celebrated by many HCR people. Although HCR apartments did not contain telephones, the resort was not completely out of communication. For a long time, a public telephone booth stood at the entrance end of the center divider in the parking lot. Its convenience for communication was apparently strongly outweighed by its nuisance value, which was the result of its use for numerous long and loud conversations. "Somebody on the phone would yell, like they're talking to New York, and everybody could hear them," according to Aggie Parlee. The phone was also allegedly used for questionable purposes. The resort had the phone company remove the booth in 1997.

A new telephone on the lanai of the office was installed, but this also suffered from the same phenomenon: the farther away your listener was, the louder you had to talk. According to Marion Burns, "It's a long way back to New York." She also recalls that there were long lines. "If you were still working in your office and you had to call New York, you had to get up pretty early and get down to that phone." And you had to talk loudly too! But at least the new phone was out of the rain.

In 1999, a plan was developed to make the approach to the pool area "more gracious," in the words of Janne Hayward. This plan envisioned an "oriental theme" bridge leading across the stream from the parking lot to the recreation area, with a twenty-by-forty-foot covered patio area called the gazebo to be located between the stream and the pool. The old ice house/laundry shed was to be removed. Complications arose, however, since construction would involve part of Charo's property, and there were other construction expenses with a higher priority. As of this writing, this plan has not yet been carried out. Such a project has been suggested several times since, and there is still a desire to build a bridge to the pool.

In 2000, a proposal was made to beautify the entrance to the parking lot by building a lava stone structure to hold the signs and, possibly, a Hawaiian hut that might be used as a lei shop. This plan was also not implemented, partly due to safety concerns and partly to competing needs; however, the board did contract with Tommy Taylor to complete a less expensive planting that would enhance the appearance of the entrance and improve visibility.

One addition to the resort was small in scope but contributes nicely to the resort's atmosphere. In 2003, a committee led by Mary Neudorffer selected names for each building. Each name is a Hawaiian plant, animal, place, or cultural term, and the first initial of each name matches the letter designation of the building. The assignment of names is based on the Hawaiian alphabet, which does not include all the letters used in English, so that *P* substitutes for *B*, *K* substitutes for *D*, *P* substitutes for *F*, *K* substitutes for *G*, and *I* or *K* substitutes for *J*. According to rental program minutes, "The intent is to enhance the ambiance at HCR, providing a softer and more Hawaiian feel to the resort. It is hoped that building names would capture some of the local lore and feeling, and help our guests and owners learn about the culture of this special island, Kaua'i, and of this area on its north shore." In 2004, ceramic plaques were placed on each building to display the name. This information is also included in the guest directory provided in each suite.

HCR's grounds are an expression of its essential nature. For this reason, it is very fitting that plantings and landscaping should be used to recognize and celebrate members of the HCR community who especially personify its spirit. Two such memorial gardens have been created.

One member of the HCR family who was much loved and missed when she passed was Bernadine "Bunny" Alexander. She served as a board member, an officer, chair of the interior and insurance committees, and a member of others. Bunny was so beloved that in 1997, HCR created a memorial garden in her name. It is in the fork in the path just before the bridge.

In 2014, owners and staff gathered in the pool and recreation area to dedicate Cissie's Garden in memory of Royce "Cissie" Meyer, who passed in 2013. Cissie was a longtime resident of the north shore and had worked at HCR since the early 1980s. She was loved especially for her enthusiastic smile and soft laugh. Cissie's Garden incorporates a new flowing water feature set among palms and floral plantings. Following a Hawaiian chant, people shared their memories of Cissie and joined in a spontaneous chorus of Pete Seeger's "Where Have All the Flowers Gone?" to celebrate the recurring cycle of life. The participants then fleshed out the garden by rooting orchids, Cissie's favorite flower, along the newly flowing water and skyward on the trunks of the new palms.

Bldg	Name	Meaning	Image
A	Ali'i	Royalty, Hawaiian Chief or Chiefess	Headress
B	Pueo	Hawaiian Owl, regarded as a benevolent 'aumakua or ancestral guardian. Seeing one is considered a good omen	Owl in flight
C	Kukui	Brought to Hawaii by the first Polynesians, the Candle Nut tree's nuts were used for oil to light torches. Other uses included food, medicine, black dye, fishing, canoe building and leis. A symbol of enlightenment, figuratively a guide or leader, in 1959, it became the official emblem of our state.	Leaf with lei and lamp
D	Koki'o	The white hibiscus, native to Hawaii, is the only fragrant hibiscus in the world.	White hibiscus with leaves
E	'Elepaio	Hawaiian Flycatcher, a small bird found in Kokee, Kauai, is believed to be the goddess of canoe makers. When found pecking slowly on a tree trunk, Hawaiians believed the tree to be insect ridden and not fit for canoe building.	'Elepaio
F	Pua	Flower, blossom; also refers to a young child	Naupaka
G	Kahili	Feather standard carried in front of royalty.	Kahili being carried
H	Hokule'a	Star of Happiness, used by Polynesians to find Hawaii. Also the Hawaiian canoe that sailed to Tahiti in 1979 using ancient navigation techniques, namely the stars and currents.	Hokule'a canoe on ocean w/star
I	'I'iwi	Hawaiian Scarlet Honeycreeper, a small red bird that lives in Kokee, Kauai. It feeds on Lehua blossoms. Feathers were used to make royal cloaks.	'I'iwi
J	'Ilima	Indigenous plant with small delicate orange flowers grows near the ocean. Used for special occasions, one lei requires 2000 flowers.	'Ilima flower w/leaves and lei
K	Kalo	Also known as Taro, is the primary food source of the Hawaiians. Leaves cooked as vegetable and its root pounded to make poi.	Kalo plant with leaves and tuber
L	Lehua	Flower of the 'Ohi'a tree, favored by Pele, famous in songs and stories. Also a small island off Kauai.	Lehua blossom
M	Mokihana	Native tree found only on Kauai, its fragrant berries strung into one of the most popular leis of Kauai.	Mokihana Lei

Names of each HCR residential building corresponding to its initial letter, along with interpretation and image to appear on building plaque, 2007. (From the author's collection)

In addition to the various changes to the overall plan of the resort, individual units have evolved over time.

Customizing

Each residential building is divided into four units, two on each floor. Each is a separate apartment—a suite of rooms. When first built, each suite contained an interior kitchen, a sitting room, a bedroom, a *pune'e* room with movable couches that could serve as additional beds, and one bathroom located off the back hallway. At first glance, all of them still look pretty much the same. But if you take a closer look, you'll notice the details that differ both outside and inside. HCR people love talking about how this came about. The changes reflect both the common values of the HCR family and the specific needs of individual owners. Much of the variation among the units reflects the personal choices of individual owners with respect to customized furniture, finishes, layouts, and artwork. But some variations have spread among the owners to such an extent that they have become structural characteristics of HCR itself. Among the primary achievements of these latter changes has been the introduction of more light and usable space. One set of improvements brought the outside inside; it brought our spectacular and serene scenery to the interior of the units.

Windows

As you walk around the resort, note how many different configurations of windows you can identify. Look for glass windows, large and small. Look for wooden louvers—single, double, or triple. Look for glass louvers. When the units were first constructed, there were no windows on the ends of any units, and there were no picture windows. "I mean, with all this scenery around, you put walls in front of it!" exclaimed Laura Richards in wonder on hearing about the early windowless units. There was a view through the sliding glass doors to the lanai, but nothing else. This lack of windows can be seen in early photographs of the resort.

To allow for air flow, there were openings with hinged wooden louvers on the front and back of the buildings. But there were no glass windows. This practice appears to have been common throughout the Islands at the time HCR was built. In some cases, preservation of the airflow produced by the louvers was more important than the view they blocked. To introduce more light into the interior while retaining the airflow from louvers, some owners switched from wooden to glass louvers. But whether they were wooden or glass, the louvers could be problematic: in heavy rain, they leaked and required constant maintenance. Averil and Howard Koch recall that Howard once had to refinish all the louvers in all the windows in the resort. This was another incentive to upgrade to well-sealed windows.

As late as 1989, glass pane windows had not yet been installed on this building, which still retains its wooden louvers. (Courtesy HCR Archives)

In the early 1980s, a few owners began installing both end and front windows in their own units. In some cases, they replaced the existing wooden louvers with new glass panes. In other cases, they installed glass panes in newly cut wall openings. Some people added only one window; others, more. Interestingly, not everyone was convinced that the addition of windows was worth it, especially where the view provided was only of other buildings or the mountains behind the resort. There was a trade-off between the enhanced quality of life and the cost. Lionel Medeiros says that his windows cost a total of about $3,000, so it was not a trivial expense. The windows also required washing, and that, too, would be an ongoing expense. Rich Sells recalls that when their windows were first installed, he and Nancee would wash the windows themselves each week so that it would not be an expense for the owners' association. And once there were windows, it was also necessary to provide shades. Still, not installing windows also had its drawbacks. There was no view, of course, and it was dark inside.

Tom Stansell recalls the process:

> I think people started putting in windows for one reason or another, and the other owners said, "Oh my gosh, what a wonderful thing." And then individually we paid for them and had them done. We had to petition the board for the right to do it, and then we paid for the windows to be installed.

Many window installations occurred during the post-Iniki reconstruction, and most were completed when buildings were taken out of service in the early 2000s. A few have occurred relatively recently. One estimate is that 150 new windows were installed in the twenty years prior to 2007. Most folks now agree that the investment in windows was well worth it to obtain the payoff of the visual experience that they enable. Installation of side and picture windows has spread to almost all units. But even so, you can pick out many variations from one suite to another: a small window there, a louver here. One apartment even had a hexagonal porthole for a while. These variations have been designed to optimize the view for the specific setting of each suite. See how many different kinds of windows you can find.

Variations in placement and choice of glass panes or wood louver windows within one building. (From the author's collection)

Kitchens

Even with external windows, it was still necessary to bring more light to the kitchens. When first built, the kitchens were isolated, dark, and claustrophobic. Not only were there no windows in the units, but the kitchens had four full, solid walls, making them feel like "a cubby hole," according to Laura Richards. Dennie Stansell remembers that "the kitchen was completely closed off. There was just the doorway opening into the kitchen. There was not the serving bar that there is now." According to Nancee Sells, "It was a solid little hot box in there. And there was no overhead lighting at first." Dark, mahogany-stained cabinets added to the gloomy atmosphere. Laura Richards says the inside was "totally dark." Several improvements brought more natural light into the kitchens and provided a greater sense of spaciousness—or at least reduced the feeling of isolation.

The first improvement was to remove part of one wall facing the hallway and bedroom and convert it into the serving bar that exists in all units today. Laura Richards reports that unit G-3 pioneered this modification, and then "everybody started going, 'Well, that's kind of cool,' so then all of a sudden we put them in every room. Those were all built by David Swenson." The resulting open-concept kitchen allows the person in the kitchen—and really, only one person at a time can fit in the kitchen—to see and engage with those in the living areas. Kitchen duty is no longer a term in isolation.

In the mid- to late 1980s, some owners also carried out a second kitchen improvement that seems to have been initiated by Robert and Nella Ebert. They moved the refrigerator and cut a pass-through into a second wall to provide more light to the kitchen. According to Rich Sells, "This pass-through was done kind of piecemeal. Before that, it was a solid wall. It was like a dungeon in the kitchen. And it was dark and hot. This change eliminated a little bit of storage, but it gave us a more open feeling to the kitchens. And we got a little bit of storage underneath." This is sometimes referred to as the Rainforth Kitchen Conversion after Dick Rainforth, who was Chair of the maintenance committee at the time. Adoption of this second change is still ongoing, spreading slowly among the apartments.

Bathrooms

While these changes provided a greater sense of spaciousness, if not actual added space, other changes did provide more usable space in the units. Most of our suites today have two bathrooms, but when they were built, they had only one. When HCR was first constructed, each suite came equipped with a stacked clothes washer-dryer setup located in a single bathroom. Given the challenge to plumbing maintenance in our environment, you might think these interior washer-dryer units would have been problematic. You would be correct.

"They had a washer and dryer. But they were nothing but trouble. Oh my gosh," says Claire Walker. And Nancee Sells remembers that Claire told her that "they're going to take the washer-dryers out because of the constant repair." So the in-unit appliances were replaced with a communal laundry facility—the Wishie Washie Hale, as the sign read—that was first located in the little hut behind the office and later in the cottage on the restaurant grounds, the present-day spa, and finally, the pool area when it was built in 1981. When the in-unit machines were removed, that space was converted into a storage closet. This closet set the stage for an even bigger transformation.

Dick Moody pioneered the two-bathroom concept. Rich Sells remembers, "Dick was the first one to put in a second bath. He just did it on his own. He said, 'I'll show you how to do this.' And he did." Dick Moody described the birth of the idea: "I was fixing my own unit, and I was talking about redoing the bathrooms. The board didn't realize it could be done. I said, 'There's enough room to do it, so why don't I just go do it?'" The board approved the modification, and Dick began the work, collaborating hands-on with the workers. His family came over to help too.

When Dick started his bathroom project in 1999, the one bathroom had a tub, and access was via a corridor along the back wall of the apartment, starting near the entrance. The bathroom contained the storage closet that was previously the in-unit washer-dryer setup. "So Dick figured out that that could be the shower," according to Dennie Stansell.

Each suite also had a separate clothes and storage closet off the room with the sliding twin beds (the *pune'e* room). The back wall of this closet butted up against the back wall of the original bathroom. Dick converted the closet off the *pune'e* room into a second bathroom by moving the back wall to the other side of the existing bathtub, thus moving the tub from the original bathroom into the new one. He then added a toilet and washstand. He also converted the closet space in the original bathroom into a shower stall; thus, he ended up with two bathrooms. The original bathroom, a little smaller than before, was now equipped with a shower, and the second bathroom, the new one, which had a tub, replaced the original *pune'e* room closet. "His genius design," Dennie Stansell calls it. "It eliminated the second closet and reduced the size of the main bathroom. After he did that, we all said, 'Hey, I want one! I want one!'" recalls Rich Sells enthusiastically. Dick was eighty years old when he completed his bathroom project.

The second bathroom generated so much enthusiasm that other owners were literally lined up on the landing outside the apartment to view Dick's installation even before the remains of the construction were cleaned up. Linda Stoskopf recalls, "It was maybe the day before the homeowners' meeting. Dad and I were working in the unit. There was a group of people lined up outside waiting to come in and look at it. So we got it cleaned and had people come in." Many owners liked what they saw and wanted to undertake a similar conversion in their own units. The two-bathroom conversion was exciting enough to earn a mention in a 2005 article about the resort in the *Garden Island*.

The Moody two-bathroom conversion was so successful that the resort management used it as the prototype to create plans for converting all the units. It was estimated that creating two bathrooms could be done for "practically the same cost as remodeling the existing bathroom." Scott Fladgard, the maintenance committee chairman, led this effort, and he included Dick Moody in the planning. Conversion of the bathrooms began in 2000 and "was a gradual process until we took all the buildings out and then did it completely," says Rich Sells. Maintenance Supervisor Steve Pastore oversaw the work. The majority of the conversions occurred during the big renovation of all the buildings that began in 2000 and lasted through 2007.

Owners agreed that the second bathroom was definitely needed. "We could hardly wait! One bathroom! You bring five people, three kids back from the beach and try to cycle them through!" exclaims Dennie Stansell. Bob Johnstone agrees, "Most units going to two bathrooms was huge. I mean, that was gigantic." Guests also appreciate having two bathrooms, as Dick Moody reports, "In my guest book, people write in and say, 'Without the second bath we couldn't have survived here.'"

There is still some variation among units, as some units are two bath, some are one and a half, some retain the old storage closet, and a few were not converted at all.

What kind of bathroom do you have? Do you know how it got that way?

A side effect of the two-bathroom modification is the Moody Closet, a small clothes closet about two to three feet square, built in the corner of the *pune'e* room. The folding louver door that separates the *pune'e* room from the living room is attached to the outside of the closet rather than to the wall. Always the handy man, Dick Moody built the first closet himself for about fifty dollars, the cost of a piece of plywood, as an alternative to the standard armoire that was on offer for several hundred dollars. The Moody Closet was a cost-effective way to regain some of the storage space lost with the second bathroom conversion. It also provided a little more privacy for the person using the new bathroom. On the other hand, some felt that it changed the distribution of light in certain units and affected the fêng shui. A few owners have copied the Moody Closet, but it has not caught on like the double bathroom concept.

Preserve and Protect

"Things that live on the beach, wooden things and metal things, suffer," says Georgia Henry with resignation. It is HCR's location, on the edge of the sea in the path of the tropic trade winds, that makes it so attractive. It is also this very location that poses a continual challenge to its structure and appearance. The water and salt from the sea are carried inland to join with the materials of which HCR is built, causing chemical reactions that damage and deface the materials and leave messy residues. This environment is harsh, sometimes surprisingly so to people used to more temperate regions. What elsewhere may require minor, casual touch-ups, here requires constant, focused, and planned efforts to preserve. These same conditions also promote the rapid growth and spread of vegetation that requires additional effort to be kept trimmed and in check. The jungle is lurking within those neatly trimmed hedges. And "creepy crawlies would come up out of the drain every once in a while," recalls Owen Paepke.

Once HCR was built, it became necessary to keep it in good repair. This is "a constant maintenance project," asserts former maintenance manager Tommy Richards.

Do It Yourself

Early on, committees composed of owners directed much of the staff activity: choosing furniture, performing maintenance, and directing grounds work. As we have seen, owners themselves were sometimes actively involved in operations, such as landscaping and construction. There are numerous examples of such volunteer work. Mary McGregor recalls that when the resort first opened, there were no plants. A friend of Mary's had a greenhouse near Kilauea, and Mary was able to move some of his plants to HCR. Averil Koch would actually go into the front office and work while she was here. Bob Johnstone recalls a visit when he and Barbara arrived to find that some vegetation had suddenly grown up so high that it was blocking the view from their second-floor lanai. The day after he reported it, he awoke to find Jack Caldwell, another owner, hacking it down with a machete. There was no planned renovation schedule, and repairs were often made only when the situation had become critical. "These units were in just sad shape. Sad shape. A lot of deferred maintenance outside and inside. It was treated like a beach house," recalls Aggie Parlee about the early days. "I wouldn't invite any guests."

Laura Richards remembers:

> Now it was very nice when Dick Rainforth and Howard Koch, they would have fun; they would get their paint, get the paint buckets out, and they'd walk around. We had no real painting system or anything, so they would just go around and look for all the places where the paint was coming off. And they'd do a little scraping and a little touch-up.

At one time, Aggie Parlee realized that her unit had inadvertently become the "chair repair shop." Whenever she visited her apartment, she found the edging trim on her chairs all torn and shredded. She would fix them up only to find that when she next returned, they were all ratty again. Eventually, she realized that between visits, the staff was replacing the repaired chairs with damaged pieces, knowing that on her next visit Aggie would repair the ones that needed it.

Averil Koch also talks about owners performing routine maintenance around the property: "They'd give me these little odd jobs to do. We had a lot of volunteer labor among the owners." As an example, she repainted the inside of a bunch of cabinets all over the resort so that they looked better. "It took me two years to do that," she remembers. These repair and maintenance efforts were in the spirit of taking active responsibility for one's own property, just as owners would do around their own full-time residences. They were behaving as if they were home. Which, in a real sense, they were.

Board members would also take on projects that were a bit more ambitious. In 1997, according to board minutes, Scott Fladgard, the chair of the maintenance committee

> took it on himself to design a new bridge, ordered timbers custom-milled and treated for our climate, and had them shipped to the premises. Scott then organized a crew of "reluctant" board members, Jack Caldwell and Fred Marotta, along with a guest of his and the assistance of an engineer guest of the resort, who spent a whole day demolishing and rebuilding the bridge.

The plan was to complete it by 5:00 p.m. so returning guests could get to their units. The "engineer guest" was Jim Thompson, who later became an owner. As Jim recalls,

> We noticed a bunch of owners with their stack of materials. They seemed to be a little puzzled as to how to take the old bridge down and put the new one in place. We were staying in H-4 at the time, so we made lunch and I took mine out to the lanai and mentally went through the bridge project. It took about forty-five minutes to fill up four sheets of paper with step-by-step instructions. I took the papers down to them and said, "I'm a guest here, and this isn't my bridge, but I am an engineer. If it were my bridge, here's how I would take it apart." They came back and said, "We like your plan, and we want to do it tomorrow. Are you available to help?" I didn't ask Carol but said yes. They went to work the next day.

The resort staff assisted with the heavy lifting of the timbers spanning the stream. According to Jim, they worked "Egyptian style," rolling the beams into place on many, many pipes. At the end of the day, the bridge was 90 percent complete and usable. After the board meetings, Jack Caldwell and Fred Marotta completed the finishing touches of routing and sanding the handrails. Carol Thompson still calls the finished product the Honeymoon Bridge, since she and Jim were actually on their honeymoon (They had been married—on the beach at HCR—a few days earlier, but that is a story for later.) when Jim's attention was diverted from his bride to his bridge. The bridge experience partly motivated Jim and Carol to buy a unit a few years later, because according to Jim, "We had been coming here for ten years, and we enjoyed it. We wanted to see it thrive and prosper."

Talking about the time that he refinished all of the window louvers, Howard Koch recalls:

> We stripped them, refinished them, and reinstalled them. This was all done with volunteer laborers. Anybody that wanted to pitch in and do it, and this is how we really took care of the place. We had a couple of maintenance programs we put in later, and we'd get fellows to come on board and commit themselves to a building at a time, and they would paint, repaint them and do this, and they'd get bored and tired after not very long, and then pretty soon we'd have to hire some guys. So it wasn't as effective as it is now. But of course, the costs went up.

Maintenance by owners was not a policy, and it was not a universal practice. It occurred when the skills, interests, and motivation of individual owners happened to coincide with some needed repair. Georgia Henry, who was manager in the early 1980s, does not recall any instances, except for the tiling of the barbecue, of owners performing maintenance work. In fact, the presence of a professional maintenance staff has always been part of the attraction of HCR. Dick Moody especially likes having someone to watch over the property because "I am not here more than I am here," quotes Linda Stoskopf. Owners do not need to spend their vacation cleaning clogged drains, replacing damaged furniture, or scrubbing floors. Molly Ksander feels that

> HCR in itself is a perfect compromise of having a place on the north shore, but living off-island. Because there's somebody there to take care of it. You don't have to board up the place or hire groundskeepers. You're on the borderline of having the ocean or the jungle take it all back. You have to be constantly keeping it dug out of nature. You arrive to fresh flowers, and white sheets, and everything clean. It's such a pleasure to walk into.

During the period when the chair of the maintenance committee played a role similar to that of a maintenance manager, HCR benefited from a succession of able volunteers, including Dick Glasier, Scott Fladgard, Dick Rainforth, and Chris Schoen, who worked well with a series of actual maintenance managers, including Bill Nelson, Rick Rodrick, Steve Pastore, Tommy Richards, and Doug Schneider. Tommy, now retired but still available to plug critical gaps, attributes the success of the maintenance program to the staff. "It is still very much an *'ohana* feeling. Everyone kind of takes care. Get the job done; it does not matter what department you are in. The feeling is that it is everybody's responsibility. 'I will help you. I got it.' Excellent teamwork."

Going Professional

Eventually, the maintenance staff came to report formally to the general manager rather than informally to the chair of the maintenance committee, and the owners gave up active involvement in ongoing maintenance activities.

In the early days of HCR, maintenance was piecemeal, performed on an as-needed basis. Over time it improved. Rich Sells recalls, "Back before we started on the building renovations, there was really no plan or anything that's organized. It was, 'OK, let's fix that; let's fix that; the building needs siding; let's do that.'" Sometimes even this was limited. According to Dick Moody, "It wasn't well run at all, it looked like a Motel 6," a comparison that came up more than once in owners' comments about the early HCR.

"It was just barely maintained; our windows leaked; it just did not seem like anything was moving forward. We were very excited when the board ultimately decided to do a lot of maintenance," says Linda Stoskopf. "It has improved. I have seen a nice difference."

Owen Paepke also applauds the improvements in maintenance. "Everybody was just sort of winging it, and they had very low expectations at the time that anybody would do anything about anything," he remembers. "When things did not work well, they just did not work. We do not so much tolerate that anymore." Comparing the resort now to when he started visiting in the early 1970s, Owen declares, "The facilities are really far, far above what was there when I started going. We need to give guests an experience that is not going to send them home with a bunch of colorful horror stories."

Owen also observes that over time, "people have done much more by way of prevention, the use of materials and components that will be hugely more resistant to the elements." The result is that there is less need to be on top of fixing things.

Efforts were also made to approach maintenance more systematically. In 1982, for example, rental program minutes mention a matrix system, and Janne Hayward recalls that a matrix system was put in place to organize the maintenance effort in 1986. Tommy Richards recalls using the system several years later:

> We used to keep track of whenever we replaced stoves, refrigerators, added fans to units. That way you could find out when each unit's fridge got changed, when the stove got changed, what units were getting changed more often—probably your oceanfront premiums on a more regular basis.

In addition, thirty-six units were systematically refurbished that year, one at a time, with each apartment requiring a week's work.

External repairs to ten buildings were made in 1987. In March 1988, management began to take one whole building at a time completely out of service and finish all necessary repairs and renovation on that building before moving on to the next. The work was performed largely by in-house staff, but some work was contracted out. New roofs on all the buildings were completed in 1989. The minutes of the owners' meeting in May 1991 reported that "[the] A building is in process to be followed by B building, which will be the last building. Following the B building, a tune up of all buildings will commence with special emphasis on windowsills." According to the president's letter in the summer of 1992, the cycle of updating all thirteen buildings one at a time had been completed. The timing set the scene for coming events. Hurricane Iniki would force HCR to switch from routine maintenance to emergency rebuilding. The story of Iniki deserves an entire section to itself. We shall explore this whole story in chapter 10.

In the meantime, by the late 1990s, many of the buildings again needed major repairs and renovations. The minutes of the rental program's 1996 members' meeting pointed out that the unremodeled kitchens and bathrooms were twenty-six years old, and the particleboard construction was generating a bad smell, while the December board minutes said that sixteen units needed new kitchens. The plumbing was thirty years old, and the bathrooms needed to be redone from scratch. Rich Sells recalls:

> That was another thing that occurred in the late 1990s, I think, when we decided that we needed to renovate the buildings. At that time, they were thirty years old, and we were piecemealing it; we'd do maybe a unit, but wouldn't do a whole building. So then, we started taking the buildings completely out of service and doing everything. Plumbing, electrical, siding, internal—whatever. They had deteriorated pretty badly.

New roof installation on building A in 1989. (Courtesy HCR Archives)

In 2003, HCR again applied the process of taking one full building out of service and completing all repairs and renovations one building at a time, rather than closing down the whole resort and doing all the buildings at the same time. This method was more practical and efficient and, therefore, more economical. In addition, some level of rental income would continue. Each building would be out of service approximately twenty weeks. The board also began investigating the possibility of, among other things, obtaining loans to fund the completion of the renovation project. Five buildings were still awaiting the two-bathroom renovation, so it was decided to apply the "one building at a time" strategy with these and then move on to the other buildings. The plan was to complete full repair and renovation on all thirteen buildings by 2007. Initially, it was hoped that increasing the reserve portion of the monthly fees could provide funding; however, in early 2006, after several options were evaluated, three loans were taken out to finance the project. A construction management firm, now called Rider Levett Bucknall, Ltd., was hired to oversee implementation of the renovation plan. (In chapter 10, we will hear much more about this firm.) In the course of detailing the plans, it was discovered that, contrary to previous information, it would be necessary to obtain building permits. Accordingly, execution of the plan was delayed until the permits were obtained. The full round of building renovations was completed in 2009. Attention then turned to routine refurbishing and maintenance, which was required due to the length of time that had passed since the start of the renovation process. In 2011, as part of the overall refurbishing of the resort, the office cottage was also renovated and upgraded to enhance the guest experience.

As of this writing, more than forty-five years have passed since HCR was born. It has changed continuously during this time. It has evolved, and it has been looked after. It provides the setting for life at HCR. That life has been rich—and it has been threatened—and it, too, has changed over time. Now we need to look at what makes HCR so vital.

Chapter 7
Talk Story—How It Came to Be

The board of directors and the senior staff are meeting to consider options for enhancing the appearance of the resort, the buildings, and the landscape. "You know," says one staff member, "this area around here has a long history. As we continue to evolve HCR, we ought to take that history into account."

"That is a great idea!" agree the others. "Let's check the library for a history book that tells all about HCR." But there was no such book on the history of HCR. So the board said, "Let's create that book." So they did. And you are reading that book.

HCR folk love tales of how the place came to be. They recall episodes of construction, threat, and rebuilding. They recall events famous in legend and history, they listen with deep interest to stories of long ago, and they speculate as to how HCR and its setting came to be as they are.

Legends tell us of Pele's action-filled visit to Ha'ena; of the Menehune, who built the ancient infrastructure that allowed the residents of Wainiha and Ha'ena to live off the resources of the *ahupua'a*; and of the hula students at Ke'e. Historical archives tell us that Naauole registered his family's house lot and taro ponds, his *kuleana*, in the *Mahele* organized by King Kamehameha III, Kauikeaouli, to ensure land and resources for his people. History tells us how communal land use evolved into private property through formation and dissolution of the Wainiha and Ha'ena Huis, and how the huis evolved as new people came to Wainiha as taro farmers, rice farmers, 'awa growers, and paniolo. Journalism tells us how McBryde Sugar Company built a dam, becoming involved in *Hui* business, and then initiated the partition of the hui that resulted in the land parcels where developers built the structure of HCR, which evolved into the resort we know today. The voices of HCR people tell us how HCR grew, how it survived threats from water and wind, how it protected itself and rebuilt itself when necessary, and how it organized itself and created new and better ways to manage its affairs, to attract visitors, and to satisfy the changing needs of its people. We can see all of this in our mind's eye.

Part of the magic of being at HCR is the sense of immersion in a web of powerful and fascinating historical forces. This history is like a cloud of ghosts swirling around us, invisible but dimly sensed. To know this history is to experience the existence of HCR in time, not just in place. It is to understand that HCR is what it is today because of what it has been in the past.

In our minds, we can walk across HCR and see a grass hale, chickens and pigs roaming loose, outrigger canoes on the beach, octopus hunters stalking the reef, taro growing in the stream, and an imu, perhaps, where the barbecue now is. We can hear the chanting of the kahuna. We can walk from the cave where Pele searched for a home, through the *lo'i* and sweet potatoes at Limahuli, past Lohi'au's house and the hula *halau* at Ke'e, and back along the beach where Taylor Campers played music, to Tunnels Beach where Captain Zodiac left for Na Pali. We can drive up Powerhouse Road to see the facility that sends power from Wainiha water to the south side operations that trace back to the first sugar plantation in the Islands. We can attend the annual meeting of the HCR AOAO, nod in recognition to residents of Taylor Camp, sympathize with the Wainiha Hui debating the water lease, provide firewood for our manager along with the Ha'ena Hui, salute Kamehameha III for confirming title to our land, and care for this land in the *ahupua'a* where we dwell.

HCR people take an active interest in this history. Bob Johnstone takes every opportunity to pursue Hawaiian music. Bob Eckert frequently travels to Kaua'i specifically to participate in cultural celebrations such as the annual Mokihana Festival. Carl Woodbury spends his spare time researching historical land records in the Kaua'i Library and the property office. He spends a lot of time talking story with many of the long-term residents in our area and has learned a lot about the local history and culture. Many owners keep books of photos and files of documents and newspapers. Janne Hayward has preserved much of HCR's history in her own archives. Indeed, at one time, Janne was offered the position of historian. This book is itself an effort to document the special coming-to-be of HCR. HCR has boxes and boxes full of history and photos, and HCR people are full of stories and memories.

Do you have any good stories to tell? What have you always wondered about? What is the most interesting thing about Wainiha, about Ha'ena, about HCR? Can you see the spirits of HCR Past?

Chapter 8

Life at the Beach

We have seen what HCR is structurally—its boards, its glass, its grass. But what makes HCR go? How does it work? The answer is: its people and their organization and their behavior. HCR is owned and operated by two organizations. The memberships of these overlap, but each organization has a separate legal status and a specific purpose. HCR operates as both a residential condominium association and a resort business—a hotel that rents rooms. These activities require separate organizations and separate procedures. Like the resort itself, both the AOAO and the rental program have changed over time to meet the evolving needs of the grounds and structures themselves and also those of the owners and the resort business.

The "Condo"

HCR is owned jointly by all members of the Association of Apartment Owners (AOAO), which was created as part of the same Declaration of Horizontal Property Regime that created the resort itself. This document included a set of bylaws that define how the AOAO is structured and operates. The bylaws describe the "nuts and bolts" of HCR's operations, as Alicia Cortrite says. In this respect, the HCR AOAO is a condominium association like any other. It is overseen by a board of directors and the usual officers selected from among the apartment owners. As with any condominium, the property has always been funded by regular monthly fees assessed on the owners. In 2008, part of the original declaration was superseded when the AOAO opted in to the state's new condominium laws (HRS 514-B) to take advantage of recent changes in these regulations. The AOAO is a communal group that owns all of the common elements of HCR, such as the external structure of the buildings, common plumbing and wiring leading to each suite, the swimming pool, the grounds, landscaping, and so on—anything that is not the personal property of individual owners and contained within the interior of each suite. Every owner of an apartment at HCR is a member of the AOAO. Each owner actually owns approximately 1.9 percent of the common property. The AOAO is collectively responsible for operating and maintaining the common elements of the property. In contrast, individual owners own 100 percent of their respective units and the contents and are responsible for maintaining and managing them.

Unlike many homeowners' associations, which hire professional property management firms, the HCR AOAO manages the property itself. This means that the board of directors oversees the staff, which is responsible for planning, maintenance, collection of fees, management of financial affairs, and so on. The value of this arrangement is that the AOAO does not have to pay out any fees to an outside management company. In 1999, the state of Hawai'i informed us that our status as a corporation had expired during the confusion caused by Iniki, so it became necessary to reestablish this. Over time, it became necessary to make several amendments to the bylaws. For example, in 2007, the owners approved changes in the bylaws that instituted term limits for board members and reduced the size of the board from nine to seven members. The number of board meetings at HCR was also reduced from four to three, with the fourth meeting being conducted by telephone and computer. These changes allowed for some important efficiencies and cost reductions. In 2011, the AOAO was approved as a nonprofit organization. Over time, the amendments to the bylaws have been consolidated into a single, updated document. Bob Eckert did three such consolidations in the 1980s and 1990s, and Alicia Cortrite did another in 2014.

The Early Days

The original owners of HCR were mostly based in Oahu. Many were realtors who bought into HCR for speculation. Accordingly, most of the early board members were from Honolulu. There was really no unified, long-term vision for the resort. Gradually, more and more units were purchased by people from the mainland. "That turnover made a big difference in how people were thinking about the resort. It wasn't investment; it became a place that you loved. That you bought because of the love of the place," remembers Rich Sells. The membership of the board changed accordingly. The AOAO then began to operate with the longer-term needs of the property in mind.

The first managers of HCR were Darrel and Gwen Heine. Since then, the list of managers includes Greg Taylor, Cheryl Fogarty, Georgia Henry, Jean Cox, Rick Roderick, Jane Yadao, and Laura Richards. There was also a series of assistant or night managers, including Pua Dorian, Edie Elwin, Robert Dickenson, Jane Taylor, Laura Check, Cissie Meyer, Laura Richards (Laura Beemer at that time), Steve Pastore (and his wife Sari), Glenda Diego, Susan Emma (the "Sheriff"), Jessi Anderson, and Joe Shannon (with his wife Heather and a lot of help from their daughter, Arlo). All of these people have contributed to HCR, and many, having become firm friends of owners, are the subject of entertaining stories that are fondly retold today.

Mary McGregor gleefully relates an example. She and Dave, her husband, were arriving from the mainland. Dave called the resort to let the staff know that they would be arriving late, but that since they had their own key, they could let themselves into their suite. But the manager, for whatever reason, didn't relay this information to her husband. Mary and Dave arrived around 10:00 p.m. and let themselves in.

> We came in here and took off our clothes. There was no one else around. I was in the bathroom, and I heard something. I looked out. Dave had taken off his clothes and there was a guy with a big pistol inside the unit. The

guy said, "I'm an ex-marine, and I know how to use this." And Dave said, "I'm an ex-marine, so put that damned thing away." They each said, "You are?" and they sat down and talked marine stories.

Poor Mary had to come out of the bathroom with a towel wrapped around her and close the sliders so she could put some clothes on. When Mary was dressed, Dave was allowed to go get his clothes on too. He fixed a couple of scotches—the gun stayed on the table—and they had "a lovely evening."

General managers were short-term and, for the most part, untrained. As a result, they did not promote a long-term vision for the property. To fill this gap, some owners took an active role in operating and maintaining the property; however, over time, management became more professional, and direct involvement of owners decreased. There were several reasons for this. The specific interests and skills of individual owners changed through the years, so their activities changed accordingly. The needs of the moment changed, and there was an increasing awareness of the need for special property management expertise. In 1984, for example, Marion Burns, the president at that time, made it clear that board members may not, among other things, "assume any of the authority of the manager."

Getting Strategic

In 2006 and 2007, the operational roles and responsibilities of the general manager were further clarified and strengthened, and the role of the board as a policy, advisory, and oversight body was made explicit. "This really made HCR more proficient as an operation," says Rich Sells. The board deliberately aimed at more professional and long-term management. For example, as of 2014, the general manager has been in place for twenty-one years.

According to Laura Richards, "As we were growing the business, things had started changing and getting a little more uniform." The board also made an effort to move toward a more contemporary strategic and proactive governance system. Over time, a number of formal documents and procedures were developed to assist in long-term thinking. These included formal reports to aid planning and funding of long-term maintenance and replacement needs, insurance and emergency plans, and an ongoing strategic planning process. In 1996, the long-range planning committee was formed. Since then, maintenance has improved, according to many owners, and there is much less deferred maintenance.

In 1973, the hospitality consultant, Horst Frank, set out to identify a bookkeeper for HCR. In December, Janne (Watt) Hayward was hired to take responsibility for monthly bookkeeping and financial reports. Prior to that, "They had an accountant in Honolulu, and they needed someone closer by that had more time to spend than the guy they sent stuff to in Honolulu," she recalls. At first, Janne's business, The Bookkeeping Company, worked out of an office in Lihue in what are now the county offices. In 1982, to support her bookkeeping, Janne bought HCR's first computer, an IBM PC, with the help of Jerry Routon and Bob Ebert, owners who worked for IBM. In 1992, Janne married Bill Hayward, one of the owners and a board member from 1985 to 1992. When her husband retired, Janne continued to handle monthly bookkeeping and financial reports for HCR from her home in Bozeman, Montana. Janne's contributions continue to this day. During her relationship with HCR, she was involved in many important events and was familiar with many in the HCR community. Importantly, her marvelous memory and her copious records of those times have contributed mightily to this history. In 2006, the board contracted with Christine Thies to serve as our accountant. Our accounting processes and software were also updated. Michael L. Carlsson took over from Christine in 2014.

In 2006, the mission statement for the AOAO was "Properly maintain, insure, and operate HCR in a manner conducive to the private enjoyment of the individual owner." As of 2013, this had been refined to "Operate the HCR property in a manner conducive to the owners' enjoyment and investment in a safe, secure, sustainable, and cost-effective fashion, while maintaining HCR's unique identity." This refinement was intended to expand strategic thinking and to ensure that the longer-term interests of HCR and the essential character of the resort were protected.

The "Resort"

A few owners live at HCR year-round. But many owners personally reside in their units only part time and rent them out to temporary vacationers the rest of the year. Most HCR owners participate in a vacation-rental business, the rental program, which is responsible for all the activities that are necessary for renting, servicing, maintaining, and marketing the units placed in the program by participating owners. Those owners who are part of the rental program are members of the business and share in the rental income and the costs of operating the rental business. Since it is not always obvious on a day-to-day basis, it is worthwhile to remember that members of the rental program are owners and operators of a small business—like a retail store or a neighborhood restaurant—with all of the same responsibilities, problems, and benefits. As one member said, "We are in the hotel business."

The owners of units at HCR have rented them out since the project's beginning. The way the owners recruit guests, provide services, and collect rents has changed considerably over time, however. At first, each owner independently solicited rentals and interacted directly with guests to schedule their stay and collect payment. There was competition among owners to rent their own units preferentially. The staff in the office sometimes acted on behalf of individual owners to rent each apartment, and owners would put more or less pressure on the staff to rent particular units. There are stories of owners who placed signs in the parking lot to advertise their individual units. Individual owners also provided all interior furnishings and were responsible for cleaning and maintaining their own rental units. Business was apparently not brisk. Dick Moody recalls those early days:

> We'd drive up there and spend a week or so, before I owned anything. I could walk in there and get any room I wanted. Maybe of all the units, there weren't more than half a dozen rented at a time. It was virtually empty all the time. It was not really inviting, but it was the only place to stay at that end of the island. And it wasn't occupied. I could've stayed in any building in the place. If I wanted to pay cash, I got a unit for thirty or forty dollars a night.

Life at the Beach | 109

Compilation of six postcards used by HCR for promotion over the years. (Courtesy Janne Hayward)

Competition was limited, especially on the north shore. When it was first built, HCR was one of only a few vacation accommodations on the island. There were the Coco Palms and Kaua'i Beachboy in Wailua, the Waiohai and Po'ipu Beach Hotel in Po'ipu, the Kaua'i Surf and Kaua'i Inn at Lihue, and the Hanalei Plantation Hotel at the Hanalei River mouth. "The guests were a bit more rustic group than they are today," says Owen Paepke, recalling the early years. "There were some surfer dude kind of people and there were some hippie kind of people." The people coming to HCR have changed since then, because "back then people going to the north shore really had to seek it out. Now it is way more accessible. We make it as easy as possible for people to get there."

The name Hanalei Colony Resort appears to have been used from the earliest days to help build an association between the resort and the better-known town of Hanalei in the minds of potential owners and guests. Thanks to the foresight of Ed Sokolski and Rich Sells, the name Hanalei Colony Resort was trademarked in 1986. This act strengthened the resort's brand, and it prevented other hotel operations on the north shore of Kaua'i from using a name too similar to ours. This action proved valuable in 1989 when HCR was able to convince Radisson Hotels not to use the name Colony Resort Collection for any properties between the Princeville Airport and the end of the road, thus preserving HCR's local brand identity.

The Rental Program

Beginning in 2001 and continuing into the present, the rental program has been known as HCR Associates, LLC, or HCR Associates (or just HCRA for short) and is organized as a limited liability company. What had been the board of directors became the managers, who were selected from among those owners who are also members of the business. In earlier days, other names were used, and different organizational structures were in place. For a time, the rental program was simply referred to informally as "the resort," to distinguish it from the AOAO, which was referred to as the "condominium association" or, informally, "the condo."

In the 1980s, a resort management committee oversaw the rental program, which was governed by a document called "Rental Program Procedures and Policies." In 1991, HCRA was organized as a general partnership and took over the responsibilities of the resort management committee, and the "Procedures and Policies" document was amended accordingly. HCR Associates reorganized as HCR Associates, LLC, as of January 1, 2001, to take advantage of the reduced liability provided by this structure. Since then, the rental program has been governed by a legal document called the "Operating Agreement for HCR Associates, LLC." In 2007, the rental program's operating agreement was amended to match the changes in the AOAO bylaws. Changes included fewer board members, term limits, and reduced meeting travel. Further changes have been made from time to time as needed.

Around the beginning of 1973, Kathy Scesney, who was then the president of the board of directors of the AOAO, hired a hospitality consultant named Horst Frank to improve the efficiency of the rental process for all of the units. One proposal was to hire an outside firm to manage the rental process. (It is said that Marriott Corporation was once considered.) This option has been revisited from time to time—in 1993 for example—but it has never been thought to be attractive. One reason is that such management firms make their profit by taking a significant percentage of room sale income for themselves, thus materially reducing the profit to the owners. Therefore, it has been decided that the owners/members should manage the rental program themselves. They do this through a staff that is partially shared with the AOAO.

The consultant, Horst Frank, developed a method for pooling the rents across all of the units. This was the first rental program. The original plan called for two tiers, or categories, of rental rates: thirty and thirty-five dollars per night. Forty-seven units participated in this program. In December of 1973, an improved rental program was put in place. This was developed by Jerry Routon, an owner and, later, board president, who worked for IBM and had an accounting background. The revised rental program identified three types of rental units with different rates. It used a formula to distribute the revenue from rents for each unit as well as the costs of maintaining the units for rent. This formula was, and is, based on the type of unit, the number of days each unit was available to be rented out, and the number of days that it was actually rented. A goal of this formula was to ensure that what the owner of a unit received from the total revenue pool was proportional to what the unit contributed to the pool. This method proved very satisfactory and, with slight adjustments from time to time, is still in use more than forty years later. The adoption of this revised accounting method was also the occasion when the rental program began to assume responsibility for maintaining and furnishing the interiors of the units and for marketing. In 1981, the board hired Wayne Williams as a consultant to help with marketing, to review financial statements, and generally to assist the then-manager, Georgia Henry, with the rental program. In the early 1990s, a fourth category of rental unit, premium ocean front, was added to the distribution formula to take advantage of the enthusiastic preference of guests for these units.

Most owners of HCR units are also members of the rental program. These two interests can sometimes present conflicts. What a person might want as a resident owner may not be the same as what she or he would prefer as a member of the rental business. One way to see how this interaction works is to look at the process of furnishing and decorating the units. For example, as a resident in an apartment, an owner might prefer comfortable, overstuffed furniture and abstract art, while renters of this suite might expect bamboo furniture covered with floral fabric and seascapes on the wall. It is also likely that this contrast will be different for each owner. Hotels make a serious effort to furnish all units identically in order to create a uniform look and feel that defines the property's level of quality and its brand. These, in turn, determine how much rent the hotel can charge. By contrast, in most condominium projects where each owner rents his or her apartment individually and in competition with other units in the project, there is wide variation in the style, quality, and condition of the interiors, so a prospective guest cannot be confident that the suite he or she rents will match expectations. This uncertainty limits the amount of rent individual units can charge.

To resolve these conflicting needs, HCR's rental program works with the AOAO to offer the individual owners/members a small range of furnishing options that are professionally designed to work well together in order to meet the needs of both the rental program and the owners. The resulting consistency gives guests confidence in what they will receive and justifies the level of rent being charged, while simultaneously satisfying the tastes and preferences of individual owners. This procedure balances conflicting needs between individual owners and the rental program, but it also makes it more complicated to provide a consistent, high-quality guest experience and, therefore, to enable optimal rental income. It requires that owners/members agree on the furnishings to be provided, and this often requires trade-offs and compromise in the selection process. It also requires relying on recommendations from professionals in the hospitality business who have an understanding of the desires of renters. Similar considerations apply to other community decisions, such as grounds, amenities, and even long-term visions for the resort. The effect of such a strategy is illustrated by a 1984 comment by Tuni Woodrum, an executive from our advertising agency in Oahu, that by positioning ourselves as a quality resort through upgrading the units and grounds, HCR had "transcended price and become a product." Over the years, HCR has become more proficient in balancing these kinds of concerns.

Strategic Planning

Ongoing efforts have been made to bring more strategic thinking to bear on the rental program. In 1985, it was reported at the annual members' meeting that progress had been made against the 1981 Master Plan, which was the basis for the program's business and marketing strategies. In 1990, Jane Yadao, general manager at the time, proposed creating a mission statement. In 2006, the mission statement for the rental program stated, "To maximize the profit of the individual members—specifically, in the business of resort operation." The vision statement in 2011 read, "Creating timeless memories through meaningful connections with our guests, associates, and community." This was to be achieved through living values: hospitality and service that reflect Hawaiian culture; meaningful connections with ʻOhana, ʻaina, guests, associates, and community; building community through education, green choices, and respect; promoting sustainability through internal and external long-term relationships; and producing a consistent high level of results. As of 2013, the rental program mission statement explicitly reflected the desire to balance the interlocking relationships created by HCR as both a residential property and a business, while respecting the values and history of the surrounding area: "Operate the resort business to maximize sustainable profit while retaining HCR's unique identity, in consonance with AOAO values and interest, as well as those of the local community and its heritage."

Operation of the rental program has become more professional over time. Discussing this evolution, Alicia Cortrite says,

> It's certainly much more formal. We have a much larger operation these days. It didn't used to be that way, and we weren't renting as much as we are. Certainly it's much more of a businesslike way, which is not to say that that's a bad thing, just very different.

Cover of HCR brochure in 1978. Sign at entrance advertises the Anchorage restaurant. (Courtesy HCR Archives)

The professionalization extends to maintenance and the staff. Alicia agrees that the quality of maintenance of the grounds and buildings has also improved: "I think we have people now who expect the sliding doors to work all the time. They didn't used to, and that was just OK.

But now it's not OK anymore." Carl Woodbury adds that this improvement in quality extends to the staff. "I'll tell you, the front office has just been a real treat. I think our front office now is way more customer- and owner-friendly than it's ever been."

Marketing

A successful hotel sells rooms. To sell rooms, marketing is necessary. HCR's marketing program has expanded and evolved over time to accommodate changes in the hospitality business, the local environment, technology, and increased marketing expertise on the part of HCR's staff and board. In 1976, Ted James, who had just purchased the fee simple rights to the land as well as several unsold units, seemed to have been personally involved in marketing the resort. However, in the early days, we relied heavily on outside hospitality consultants and publicity agents. Horst Frank and then Wayne Williams were consultants. They were actively involved, attended board meetings, and provided valuable guidance, both strategic and tactical. At various times, we relied on Bob Kovar on Oahu, Jarvinen & Associates in Los Angeles, DiCarlo & Woodrum in Honolulu, and Loomis and Pollock in Honolulu for public relations, advertising, and marketing services. Since 1994, Candy Aluli has been our publicity agent. By 1998, advertising was being done in-house by Laura Richards; Chris Bryan, our wedding coordinator; Vicky Golar, our webmaster; and their successors. In 2000, Debra Jason prepared a detailed marketing plan. Later, she also contributed to our Internet presence. Replacing the professional advertising agency with the in-house team had a noticeable effect—by 2000, owners noticed that bookings had increased substantially.

Throughout the years, HCR deployed a variety of promotional techniques that were typical for the time: car packages, magazine ads, trade shows, golf packages, and videotapes. Brochures and postcards have long been ubiquitous. Sometimes the resort benefited from more general publicity. In 1983, the state of Hawai'i produced a TV ad starring Carol Burnett. When Charo's Restaurant first opened, the accompanying national TV publicity resulted in a noticeable increase in HCR revenues. HCR has also offered special promotions: such as HCR's Thirtieth Anniversary, Explore

Na Pali, and Romantic Honeymoon packages. Golf packages were useful tactics, especially with the development of the Princeville courses in the 1970s and 1980s. In 1985, in support of our golf program, HCR participated in a golf tournament, the Bob Hope Navy Relief Classic. A stay at HCR was part of the prize. Alan Shepard, the astronaut, won the prize, and HCR gained valuable publicity. Also in 1985, we began the practice of holding continental breakfasts at the pool. Continental breakfasts and Mai Tai Nights have been popular ever since.

HCR rate card and special rate plans in December 1981. (Courtesy HCR Archives)

In 1994, Laura Richards began organizing Hawaiiana and keiki (child) programs for our guests. Two years later, some staff took classes in Hawaiian history at a community college location near the resort. Rekha Sharma, HCR's full-time social director, began offering a variety of Hawaiiana and keiki activities in 1998, including lei making, hula, painting, weaving, and storytelling. These were a great success. In 2001, they received a mention in the *Garden Island*. The keiki program was particularly effective in stimulating family visits. *Hawai'i* magazine quoted Laura Richards as saying, "We can have as many as forty-five children running around." To keep the kids busy, HCR once bought little fishnets for all of them and set them to catching frogs!

In 1999, HCR was deploying a seven-point marketing program, consisting of media, web, public relations, direct mail, sales representatives and wholesalers, cooperative programs, and special events. As part of this program, HCR also began its in-house wedding planning program that year. Even earlier, though, in 1997, Carol and Jim Thompson may have been one of the first couples to have been married at HCR. They had both a traditional and a Hawaiian ceremony on the beach in front of unit I-1. "It wasn't more than about three years later when weddings here on the beach were starting to get commonplace," says Jim. "We think maybe we started the 'wedding on the beach' revolution." Indeed, by 2000, HCR's wedding business was notably expanding, and Deanna Cook joined HCR as its first full-time wedding coordinator.

In 1999, the special events effort was particularly enhanced by an agreement with Surts on Beach, the restaurant next door to HCR at the time, to use food from the restaurant along with meeting space there to stage a variety of special events such as weddings, gourmet meal events, Monday night football, special theater events, and general meetings. Also in 1999, HCR joined with three other smaller, intimate hotels on Oahu, Maui, and the Big Island to form a cooperative marketing group called Hideaways Hawai'i, which was founded to "emphasize the charm and friendly ambiance that is unique to their properties." In 2001, the rental program adopted a tag line to help define our brand by unifying our marketing activities and image; this was the first use of the now-familiar "Unspoiled. Unplugged. Unforgettable." In 2002, a guest computer for Internet and e-mail access was provided in the Makana Room, and in 2011, HCR made Wi-Fi available in units and at the pool. In 2013, HCR began offering a van service to transport owners and guests to the beaches at Tunnels and Ke'e during the day and also to Princeville and Hanalei in the evening.

Technology

The front office is responsible for implementing much of the rental program's strategy and tactics; however, the front office has not always been worker-friendly. Cissie Meyer remembers working in the office in the mid-1980s, before it was fully computerized:

> So, back when I started at the desk, we did everything manually. The women I was working with, they were secretaries. They would sit down and type letters on a typewriter. And we had to do a daily audit on a pegboard to the penny. So, we were auditors and secretaries and filing clerks. I never wanted to be a secretary. So I was very, very excited when we computerized.

Laura Richards recalls that "before we had computers, we just made reservations in the office or when travel agents would call and book on behalf of clients." For years, all deposits were made by mailing a check to the office. "We did not take credit cards for deposit, but you could pay the remainder of your bill here. We ran it through one of the little handheld swipers and took all the transactions to the bank."

Scott Fladgard, the chair of the maintenance committee, personally installed the office computers in 1994. HCR's marketing and reservation technology then improved by stages with the introduction of Internet connectivity and the building of a website. Many of these developments occurred under the leadership of Tom Stansell, who was chair of the marketing committee for much of this period. Over time, the website was modernized and streamlined. Increasingly, marketing and reservations have moved to being web-based to take advantage of current travel practices. In 1988, our best source of business was our 800 number. In early 1996, we received an average of two inquires per day from our e-mail address. In early 1997, we obtained the www.HCR.com web address, and Scott Fladgard installed new computers in the office with reservation and database software. *Hawai'i* magazine said that HCR's "dandy new home page [is] almost as refreshing as an actual visit." In February 1998, Laura Richards was able to report, "We have received some bookings from our website."

In May of 1999, Tom Stansell, as chair of the marketing committee, began to look into installing a system that would allow guests to book reservations through the web. He anticipated even then that direct online reservations would become a major source of bookings. By September 1999, the website was updated to include key words designed to enable web search engines to find our site. In early 2011, for the first time, a link to HCR's website appeared on the first page of responses when "Kaua'i Resorts" was entered into Google's search window. This made it much more likely that the searcher would find HCR and actually make a reservation. HCR continues to improve the efficiency of its search engine optimization, or SEO, and exploits a variety of sophisticated web-based marketing techniques as they emerge.

HCR's online presence expanded rapidly. According to Laura, "When we first started with online reservations, we still had only about 5 percent of bookings online, exactly what was predicted in the rest of the world at that time." In February 2000, 20 percent of our bookings were made through the website, and in 2014, the figure was more than 50 percent. The rest are by telephone. In 2011, we made it possible to book directly through personal mobile devices such as smartphones and tablets. In early 2012, HCR was present in all social media, and in 2014, the website was refreshed so that it has a consistent look on different kinds of electronic devices.

Not everyone is online, however, even in today's world. In 2014, Laura got something surprising in the mail. "I received a letter from a man asking for information about the resort and pricing. I was so amazed, since I doubt we have seen that in many years! I almost did not know what to do."

One of the services provided by online travel websites is a system of informed ratings of the quality of vacation properties. Expedia, the Internet travel website, uses a five-point scale. Following a visit to HCR in 2013, Expedia raised their rating from three stars to three and a half stars out of five and informed us that they believe that certain improvements could make HCR a four-star property. At the same time, HCR was rated 4.6 out of 5 by guests who provided comments on Expedia.

As HCR's online presence expands, so does its active guest community, which intermingles with each other and with the staff through modern social media and online travel sites. The social media environment is like a giant communal guest book where guests can share their comments with HCR and with each other. On a recent Thursday morning, for example, a guest posted a photo of the view from the window of her suite on a social media site. Within minutes, others responded that it reminded them of their stay at HCR, while still others said they were looking forward to visiting for the first time. One person asked which suite it was, and a staff member identified it, with the result that still more people said they remembered staying in that exact suite. Within two hours, there were ten lengthy comments and forty-three people had "liked" the photo. At the same time, on one travel site, there were 229 reviews of HCR by guests and 190 photographs. A recent TripAdvisor review by Rich Sells received more than 2,100 visitors! Social media has created a guest book with a difference! Guests and staff share their comments continuously in real time, so that the guest book has become a guest (and possible guest and owner and staff and travel professional) conversation.

An important part of the HCR experience for guests and owners is the array of nearby amenities they can enjoy during their stay. These amenities do more than simply provide enjoyment—they help define the very appearance and experience of HCR. We have heard the story of HCR's swimming pool and barbecue areas; however, some of the most significant sources of comfort and pleasure for the HCR community are not strictly part of HCR but are, nevertheless, intimately united with HCR.

A Destination

An important, even critical, component of the rental program's strategy to attract guests is the complex of businesses that are linked to HCR. The restaurant, the gallery and coffee shop, and the spa make

HCR not just a cluster of transient vacation rental units, but a full-service resort—a destination. William Stewart, who operates the Na Pali Art Gallery and Coffee House says, "All the businesses complement one another; we all help each other out. So it's a really nice synergy that we have going."

In addition to their value in attracting guests, these businesses—especially, perhaps, the restaurant—also provide significant value directly to owners who rely on the ability to "run next door" for a gourmet meal and an evening's entertainment or a deep massage. It also provides space for meetings of the owners' association and rental program. Prior to the availability of space in the restaurant, annual meetings were held in a variety of rented off-site venues, such as the Princeville Country Club, Hanalei Bay Resort, Wai'oli Mission Hall, and even Tahiti Nui. There may be a tendency to take the restaurant, spa, and gallery/coffee shop for granted, but history shows that this is false confidence.

The Restaurant

The restaurant next door to HCR is another of those fabled locations that is the setting for many happy and significant occasions for HCR and its extended family. From its beginning, the development project included a restaurant structure. There has always been a restaurant building next to HCR; however, there has not always been a restaurant operating in the building. When there was a restaurant, it was not always the same one. And the restaurants that were there were not always what they might have been or what the HCR community would want them to be. But the restaurant facility has always been a vital part of the HCR experience and a celebrated source of memories and stories.

The Anchorage. When Sherman Dowsett began development of HCR, he also acquired the adjacent lot (which had been lot 76B when the Wainiha Hui was dissolved) for the construction of a restaurant that opened in 1969. At first Dowsett operated a bar and restaurant known as the Anchorage (although photographs and stationery show that the official name was "the anchorage," in lowercase letters). The shoreline just north and west of the restaurant is called Anchorage Point. A passage through the reef allows small boats to reach the shore.

It is tempting to speculate that the name of the location is somehow related to the practice of anchoring vessels here, in particular traditional fishing boats. Laura Richards recalls that at one time boats participating in an ocean yacht race from Australia would anchor there, just outside the reef. Edie Elwin, who would be HCR's assistant manager in the late 1980s, acted as shore liaison for this race, maintaining radio communication and announcing when the boats were coming. Sailors from the anchored racing vessels frequented the restaurant. The Anchorage offered a steak and seafood menu and provided live music. On the seaward side of the restaurant, there was an open terrace. In the early 1970s, Fred Morris was manager of the Anchorage, and Pua Dorian, known as Rose, was his assistant. At one time, the Anchorage was managed by a local woman, Cathy Ham Young. (Later, she provided flowers for HCR units and special events.) The Anchorage was a favorite hangout for Ha'ena residents, including Taylor Campers and HCR owners. Claire Walker, for example, remembers often staying until closing time.

The Sandgroper. The next incarnation of the restaurant was the Sandgroper. In 1978, Ted James, who had purchased the restaurant from the developer Sherman Dowsett, sold the restaurant property, including the parking lot and cottage (now the spa) to Colin Forbes. Forbes and his wife, Kathy, came from New Zealand and had connections to Australia. They then operated it under the name the Sandgroper. (A sandgroper is a type of burrowing insect in Western Australia, but it is also a slang term for beachcomber.) Dick Moody describes the restaurant: "They cooked one turkey a day, and when the turkey was gone, they closed. They had a very small menu because this man and his wife and one cook ran the entire place. That whole back end was just an open patio, with a big barbecue going, so you'd barbecue whatever you wanted done."

Forbes remodeled the building and enclosed the seaside patio area. The location of this area can still be detected by the slightly lower floor level in one corner of the restaurant. According to Howard Koch, "Colin Forbes was a character. He ran a good bar. He couldn't make it go as a restaurant, so they used to have pupus—no real meals, just appetizers."

And, according to Averil Koch, "good booze. We had a good relationship, and when he'd close at night, that's when we'd go over and play cards."

A travel writer described Forbes and his wife as "a joint enigma unlikely to leave many guests without some sort of reaction. Most people love them. Some don't stick around in the pub long enough to realize that Colin's outback Australian humor and gruffness is only a front for a rare and colorful individual." Forbes and his wife lived in the small building that now houses the Hanalei Day Spa, so they were around HCR much of the time. Georgia Henry recalls going to the pool to lock up one night about 10:00 p.m., and "as I walked in, there was a great big party going on there. It was Colin Forbes and about eight other people. Well, his wife was there, too. All of them were stark naked, having a barbecue." Forbes became ill after several years, and in 1985, he and his wife sold the restaurant to Charo's corporation and returned to their native land.

Charo's. Charo had fallen in love with the Ha'ena area when she honeymooned there with her new husband, Kjell Rasten. She soon bought a home in Ha'ena. In 1989, *Kauai Business and Real Estate* reported that the restaurant at HCR had fallen on hard times by 1985 and that Charo bought it as a "challenge." Dick Moody recalls that before opening the new restaurant, Charo hosted televised beauty contests there. "I think she performed. She led into the programs that she was having photographed. Her picture was always there with all these beautiful women standing up being judged."

Charo is a character—one of a kind and a force of nature. She is the archetype for a whirling bundle of energy. She may be most familiar from her numerous appearances on *The Tonight Show* (with Johnny Carson) and *The Love Boat*. Charo is a musician, a singer, a dancer, a comedian, an actor, a nightclub performer, and a reality show star. She records in pop, Latin, flamenco, and classical guitar styles. And she is a powerful businesswoman. No one who has met her will ever forget her. And they all have a story. Marion Burns recalls that "she was very good in her business dealings. She was a nice woman." Alicia Cortrite recalls meeting her while Charo was operating the restaurant. "I have met Charo, yes, when she used to be there fairly often. That impression that you get never leaves your mind once you've met Charo."

Charo is also generous. Tom Stansell remembers that when meeting Charo for court hearings in Honolulu, "she just waited for court because she was handing out money to every bum along the sidewalk on her way to court." Laura Richards recalls that after settling a liquor license issue with the county, Charo made a substantial donation to Hanalei School. She has had, and continues to have, a significant impact on HCR.

Charo expanded the restaurant space. After the initial renovation in 1985, Charo's Restaurant & Bar (sometimes called Charo's Cantina but mostly just Charo's) could seat 160 people for lunch and averaged one hundred reservations. It reportedly had a staff of sixty. Charo operated the restaurant for a number of years, serving a variety of menus and formats. She herself would perform for the guests, and she also provided a variety of music. Chuck Williams recalls that he and Moreen met her one night. "Charo was actually in the restaurant that night, and we ordered her 'famous paella.' She brought her guitar out and played a couple of numbers." Georgia Henry recalls that Charo "did what she did very well. She would walk into the restaurant and just start at one end of it, and work her way around, and greet everybody, and stand up and have pictures taken with everybody that wanted to. And she was very charming." Charo's also offered a lu'au. It once presented a lu'au that was attended by the mayor of Kaua'i along with fifty million viewers of the television show *Lifestyles of the Rich and Famous*. The restaurant was very popular. Buses would bring in loads of customers. "It was the happening restaurant," says William Stewart.

Charo and HCR got together to agree on appropriate restrictions on hours and types of music and other arrangements to minimize noise and disturbances. Rock or disco would not be allowed. At one point, in 1988, Charo proposed adding a separate 2,900-square-foot theater adjacent to the restaurant that would seat 125 people. After eating, the restaurant patrons would retire to the theater for an evening of live entertainment consisting of flamenco, Polynesian, or Latin music and dancing. The theater would be soundproofed to avoid disturbing the neighborhood. The County Planning Commission discussed the proposal at length, and many local residents provided comments. Not all residents were opposed. One reported that after Charo had taken over the bar and restaurant, the noise problem had actually decreased, and there were fewer disturbances in the area. This respondent also was glad that the area could still have the convenience of a local restaurant. The county council approved the theater, but it was never built. According to Laura Richards, zoning requirements would have required the theater to have been built on stilts, and Charo did not like this design. Charo's Restaurant ceased operating on Christmas Day 1995, but Charo retained ownership and leased operation of the restaurant to several businesses—with varying degrees of success and some drama.

North Shore Grill. In the spring of 1997, Charo leased the restaurant to new operators who opened the North Shore Grill. In order to secure transfer of the liquor license from Charo, the operators agreed to a series of restrictions to control noise and safety issues; however, in late summer, there was a fire in the restaurant, and North Shore Grill closed.

Na Pali Prime Grill. In early 1999, Charo leased the property to the Texas Tractor Company, with Na Pali Prime Grill as a business name. According to the opening press release, this was to feature "Texas grain-fed beef, raised especially for the restaurant on a private ranch in Amarillo." Soon after the opening in March 1999, an "alarming series of events" caused Charo to question whether this was an appropriate tenant. The situation was described in the AOAO minutes for May 1999:

> Shortly after the restaurant opened, the manager quit, and the chefs were left in charge. They quit and left a long letter charging the operators with fraudulent practices. Several employees were paid with checks that bounced. It was difficult to determine who was in charge. There were demonstrations in the parking lot by disgruntled employees, drinking in the parking lot and no security provided. The AOAO decided to join Charo in the effort to deny the transfer of [her] liquor license [to Na Pali Prime Grill] and hired our local attorney to represent our interests.

The commission denied the transfer of the liquor license. The restaurant was then only able to operate without serving liquor. The result was that the Na Pali Prime Grill was not able to survive, and the restaurant closed in May 1999. It also turned out that there was some question as to whether the "special, Texas-raised beef" ever really existed.

Surts on the Beach. Next came Surts on the Beach, along with the Steam Vent Café, both of which opened in November 1999. Initially, the restaurant was open only for lunch, and in late 1999, it updated its menu and began opening for dinner. Surts was operated by Brian Crawford, who also owned the Chalet Kilauea on the Big Island, which was (and is) a sister member (along with HCR) of the Hideaways Hawai'i group of small hotels. He subleased the restaurant facility from Charo. Surts on the Beach, located in the main restaurant building, and the Steam Vent Café, in what is now the gift shop and café, were named after a restaurant and coffee shop Crawford operated in Volcano Village on the Big Island. The café did not sell any gifts or artwork. The restaurant name came from the first name of Chef Surt Thammountha, according to the *Honolulu Star-Bulletin.* Surts provided extra value to HCR by creating a special "great room" area for use by HCR guests to read, watch television, and visit. This was the Makana Room. HCR also used this space for board and owners' meetings and special events; for example, HCR threw a New Year's Eve party at Surts in 1999. Surts closed in June 2001.

HCR Associates. When Surts closed in June 2001, discussions with Charo suggested that she was amenable to leasing it to HCR. Later that year, HCR Associates, LLC, took out a one-year lease, with an option to renew for a second year, "to determine if the property can be used to enhance our rental operations through its use for receptions and group meetings of resort guests." According to *TravelAge West,* HCR now "features 2,500 square foot of kitchen and 3,000 square foot of dining and meeting space...including a lounge area with bar and cable television." Since then, HCR has either made limited use of the facility itself or subleased it to professional restaurant operators. At first, HCR did not have an operator to run the restaurant, so it used the facility for weddings, meeting space, and other special events. It also became the location for the weekly Mai Tai Parties. The *Garden Island* reported that HCR would also make the facility available for "guests of Hanalei Colony and groups and individuals who are seeking a spectacular north shore site for elegant dinners, casual gatherings, high-tech meetings, or anything in between." But the location and facilities offered by the restaurant were too valuable to be limited to HCR. So HCR looked for a new operator to sublease the restaurant.

In 2002, Louise Marston (known locally as "Auntie Louise"), who with her husband, Bruce, was the operator and the spirit of the Tahiti Nui restaurant in Hanalei, began organizing a lu'au once a week at the restaurant, with local entertainers. On occasion, HCR owner Dusty Walker, who was a professional singing cowboy on television, would sit in with them. The room was decorated with Tahiti Nui decor. With relief, owners felt that since "these activities proceed under HCR's watchful eye, past problems of noise and inappropriate behavior are no longer an issue," as Fred Marotta wrote in his presidential letter.

In early 2003, the LLC agreed to support an application by Auntie Louise to obtain a liquor license for the purpose of operating the bar in the Makana Room. Moreen Williams remembers Auntie Louise coming to their table and playing "Hanalei Moon" because she knew it was Moreen's favorite song. Tahiti Nui's connection with HCR was perpetuated for a time by the story that the Tahiti Nui sign over the doorway of the building in Hanalei was actually carved into the back of an old Hanalei Colony Resort sign left over from the days of the lu'au at HCR. HCR folks often hung out at "The Nui" (or "Da Nui")—and still do. Auntie Louise was a close friend of many HCR folk, including Mary McGregor and Aggie and Roger Parlee. Bob Eckert had become fluent in French as a result of his many years living in Europe, and Auntie Louise of course spoke French because she came from Tahiti, where French was the first language. Accordingly, Bob and Auntie Louise became *chers amis*. When Dick and Martha Moody went to eat at Tahiti Nui, they would always bring along a piece of coconut cream pie as a gift. Georgia Henry remembers, "She was a fantastic person. She traveled the world and never stayed in a hotel because she had friends everywhere." The weekly lu'au at the restaurant was discontinued in early 2004, because a reliable operator could not be found after the passing of Auntie Louise.

Tunnels Bar & Grill. In July 2004, Tunnels Bar & Grill opened in the restaurant facility subleased from HCR. The *Garden Island* reported that it was operated by William Stewart, who had been operating the Na Pali Gallery and Coffee House for about two years. The chef, formerly of the Hanalei Dolphin, offered a variety of salads, sandwiches, and entrees for lunch; varied appetizers; and meat, seafood, and vegetarian dishes for dinner. It collaborated with HCR to stage weddings. Tunnels Bar & Grill was successful, and, after about three months, William began looking for someone to take over the restaurant operation so that he could focus on the gift shop, which was his passion in life. When no successor emerged by September, Tunnels Bar & Grill closed.

Mediterranean Gourmet. In 2005, Imad Beydoun began organizing special banquets for Julie Kawagishi, our wedding coordinator at the time, and took over the hosting of the weekly Mai Tai Parties. In May 2006, the restaurant was reopened to the public as the Mediterranean Gourmet, under the auspices of Imad and his wife, Yarrow. Imad is from Beirut, Lebanon, and the menu added Hawaiian accents to a traditional Lebanese menu. Restaurant decorations were by Tommy Taylor. The Mediterranean Gourmet, or "MG" as it is called, offers a weekly lu'au and nightly entertainment, ranging from jazz guitar and Hawaiian music to belly dancing. The Mediterranean Gourmet has received a number of restaurant awards. It continues to host the HCR Mai Tai Parties and other events, such as wedding dinners, family gatherings, and occasional meetings. And there is an occasional celebrity sighting: Pierce Brosnan, of course, lives just down the road and may often be seen in the Mediterranean Gourmet. Molly Ksander remembers a Mai Tai Party one evening:

> I was standing near the bar talking to a group of guests when someone interrupted, saying, "Molly, there is someone I want you to meet. This is Pierce Brosnan." With my height, everyone is belt high to me so I just said, "Oh, good evening," to this belt and pair of shorts that looked like every other belt and pair of shorts on every other man in the place. Then I looked up at his face and

OMG! It was Pierce Brosnan! Later, at dinner, I made George sit facing their table so Pierce would not see me drooling.

Then, too, who can forget the night that Averil Koch livened up the room by joining the entertainer in performing a spontaneous belly dance with a costume sword apparently slicing through her head?

Possibilities. An operating restaurant located next door to HCR is a valuable amenity for the owners, since it provides a delightful venue for a night out with fine dining and entertainment. Who does not recall settling into the restaurant for a little "arrival night relaxation"? It is also a local gathering place, making it a fine location to meet our neighbors and learn a bit more about our spot on the north shore. For the same reasons, it is also a valuable and critical part of the resort's appeal to HCR guests, neighbors, and other visitors. HCR is remote. That is part of its attraction for many guests. But the very remoteness can be a challenge for those who do not wish to drive our north shore roads to enjoy a night out. Having the restaurant and the bar close by alleviates this problem. But in order to satisfy this need, the restaurant must be of the right sort. It must be quiet and provide an appropriate menu and entertainment. Thus it has been to HCR's advantage to support the operation of an appropriate business. As Bob Johnstone explains, "If we ever lost the lease with Charo, two things could happen: There'd be no restaurant, which would make us, again, too remote. Or she could lease it to somebody that plays rock 'n' roll music till two o'clock in the morning, and people wouldn't want to stay here." There have, in fact, been several periods in the history of the restaurant when there were serious problems with noise and disturbances around the property. These were generally resolved by discussion with the restaurant operators, but they show that there is a real risk of such problems and that control of the facility is very much in the larger interest of HCR. In addition, subletting Charo's is a significant source of revenue to members of the rental program.

In fact, several discussions of buying the restaurant facilities have taken place. Claire Walker recalls one early effort prior to Colin Forbes's acquisition of the property. Then, according to AOAO minutes from the time when Charo's closed in 1995, "some owners expressed an interest in forming a hui to purchase the facility." And again, when the North Shore Grill closed in 1997 and when the Na Pali Prime Grill closed in 1999, the HCR AOAO began discussing the feasibility of purchasing the Charo property in order to avoid "another debacle in the form of a mismanaged restaurant." The asking price was unrealistic, but there was hope for negotiation. The board authorized Laura Richards to seek permission from Charo for a formal appraisal that would serve as the basis for negotiations. Nothing came of these discussions. At one point, Rich and Nancee Sells gave thought to buying and operating the restaurant on their own. On further consideration of their lack of restaurant experience, though, they thought better of that. The idea of purchasing the restaurant has not worked out so far, but it has not entirely died away. This logic also explains why HCR continues to lease the facility from Charo and sublet it to the Mediterranean Gourmet.

Art Gallery and Coffee Shop

In the same way that HCR benefits from the presence of the restaurant, it also benefits from the other businesses associated with the restaurant property—the gift shop and the spa.

At the time that Charo operated the restaurant, she also operated a gift shop. A woman named Corky Nelson and her husband, Bill Nelson, who also worked in the HCR maintenance department, managed it. The shop sold merchandise and T-shirts emblazoned with Charo's logo. Laura Richards recalls that Corky and Bill "were wonderful neighbors and they were wonderful friends to a lot of owners here." In 1998, Charo proposed to sell packaged liquor from the gift shop. HCR resisted this, and it never did happen. The shop closed when Charo's closed. When Surts on the Beach opened, the space reopened as a sundries shop and cafe, as in many hotels, but when Surts on the Beach closed, the shop again closed. At the suggestion of Charo's sister, Laura Richards undertook a search for a new operator.

William Stewart was then living on Oahu and island hopping in search of "someplace special" to start up a gift shop. When he saw the empty space at HCR, "I scratched my head and said, 'Maybe this is it.'" He went to the office, talked with Laura, and submitted a formal business plan. "He knew exactly what he wanted to do and how he wanted to do it. He's got all the potential in the world," says Laura. So she put William in touch with Charo's organization, and he has been operating the gift shop since the summer of 2002 as the Na Pali Art Gallery and Coffee House. The gallery's offerings have become more comprehensive over time, especially with the addition of jewelry, and William continues to enhance both his offerings and the atmosphere of the site.

Day Spa

The Hanalei Day Spa, located in the cottage in the parking lot, is one of HCR's most appreciated amenities. This service began in early 2003 when the LLC accepted a proposal from manager Laura Richards to attract additional guests by offering a health spa with licensed therapists. Initially, the service was provided in a small thatched hut (hale) overlooking the beach behind the Makana Room. In early 2004, HCR subleased the cottage on the restaurant grounds to Darci Frankel to enable her to expand her spa and yoga business from the restaurant and the thatched hale facing the sea. Interestingly, the concept of a massage facility caused some concern when it was first proposed, as some board members associated massage parlors with red-light districts. The low-profile test run of the business in the beach hale resolved these anxieties. The guests reported that they loved it. And research showed that the idea of a massage and health spa was spreading throughout the Islands. So the experiment was a success, and after about a year, the spa moved into the cottage. That was around 2005. The experiment was such a success that guests now demand a spa facility. It is a huge attraction.

The amenities have always been very important for the resort guests. The combined presence of the resort, restaurant, gallery/coffee shop, and spa has been a win-win-win-win situation for all the businesses. Each draws customers who then take advantage of the other businesses. Guests often comment on how much they look forward to dining right here in the restaurant, the convenience of the coffee and pastries and gifts in the gallery, and the luxuriousness of getting a massage on the beach. Together, the four businesses are much more than the sum of their parts. Together, they provide the attraction of a full-service resort. Together, they make HCR a destination.

A Space Forever

Over the years, HCR has maintained good relations and has worked well with Charo's corporation. The two businesses have a lot in common; still, there have been a few bumps in the road. It is noteworthy that in each case, HCR and Charo's organization have continued to collaborate and do business together while resolving the issue. We have seen how HCR and Charo collaborated to deal jointly with the problem of the rogue restaurant. At another time, Charo wanted to rent the residential cottage in the parking lot to a real estate agent as an office. HCR was concerned that the demand for additional parking would cause problems for HCR guests and could result in litigation. Before anything came of this, though, Charo dropped her plan. This occurred at the same time as HCR was in legal dispute with Charo over other parking lot issues, so parking was a sensitive subject.

The most complicated, lengthy, and potentially most impactful interaction between HCR and Charo was the parking lot problem. Mentions of an issue around parking appear in AOAO minutes as early as 1985. At its core was one question: Do owners of HCR units also own the permanent right to park a vehicle in the HCR parking lot? The question had its birth in the land history of HCR. It is an interesting story, because ultimately, the root of the problem was the origin of HCR as leasehold property.

The steps that created the problem are as follows: First, the original developer, Sherman Dowsett, sold individual apartments as leaseholds, meaning that the buyers would own their apartments but only lease the land on which the buildings stood. The leases could be renegotiated for a total of fifty years, after which the right to use the land would revert back to Dowsett or his successor. Eventually, Ted James bought the fee simple ownership rights to the HCR property from Dowsett's estate, and he also bought the restaurant property. Second, over a period of several years, James began to sell individual leaseholders the fee simple rights to their units. Third, James sold the parcel where the restaurant and parking lot are located to Colin Forbes, who operated the Sandgroper. Fourth, Charo purchased the restaurant property, including the parking area, from Colin Forbes.

Over the long course of these transactions, many leases and deeds were written, and some included incorrect variations in wording about parking rights. Most of the owners' titles and title insurance policies said that they owned a permanent right to use one of the parking spaces on the restaurant property. In other words, they claimed fee simple ownership of parking rights in perpetuity, while a few deeds still included the old leasehold wording. Critically, the language in Charo's deed said that the rights of HCR owners to use any parking spaces would go away in 2024, because all the parking spaces were leaseholds, and the lease was due to expire after fifty years. Unless the leases could be renegotiated, from 2024 onward, all owners would not have the right to park automobiles in the HCR parking areas. Charo would be able to replace the parking lot with other landscaping and structures. If owners and guests lost the right to drive to the resort and park there, the value of owning a unit at HCR would decline drastically! *This* was the parking lot problem.

The issue came to a head in late 1998. At first, HCR attempted to negotiate a mutually satisfying solution with Charo. When this was unsuccessful, the HCR board of directors motivated owners to make individual claims against their respective title insurance companies. Then, through our legal counsel, we contacted those title insurance companies regarding taking legal action against Charo's corporation. Finally, HCR filed a suit against Charo's corporation, with Max Graham as our lawyer. This required that all of the owners agree to the strategy. At one point, Tom Stansell channeled Benjamin Franklin, saying, "We must all hang together, or, assuredly, we will all hang separately."

This HCR action triggered a series of events that ended with a solution to the problem. Charo countersued HCR, and then the title insurance companies on both sides became actively involved. There were many meetings and legal hearings, and eventually the matter went before a judicial mediator in Honolulu. Architects were brought in to develop a mutually acceptable plan for laying out the parking lot to accommodate the parking requirements of both HCR and the restaurant. There was a possibility of putting an end to the years of uncertainty and conflict by making a settlement in which HCR would have fewer than fifty-two parking spaces. The board and all of the owners rejected this settlement offer. Then HCR's engineering and architecture consultants developed an alternative plan for a revised layout of the parking lot, which Charo accepted. In December 2009, Tom Stansell was able to sign off on the final documents, and the parking lot problem was solved.

In the end, Charo received a satisfying financial settlement from the title insurance companies, and HCR owners received the right to park in fifty-three spaces in the lot for perpetuity. In order to accommodate all the required parking spaces, HCR had to relocate the emergency entrance to the central courtyard from between buildings B and C to between buildings C and D, in front of the office. At the last minute, thanks largely to Tom Stansell and Owen Paepke, HCR also negotiated a financial settlement from its title insurance company that could be used to pay for this relocation. In the end, this was a satisfactory outcome for all concerned. Resolution of the parking issue took a lot of time, effort, and intellectual energy on the part of a lot of people. Our attorneys ably informed and executed our strategy. The construction management firm, now called Rider Levett Bucknall, again provided valuable support. Much of the credit for the resolution goes to the HCR staff and board members who have interacted with and maintained close and friendly relations with Charo and her family throughout the years. Much credit also goes to the HCR owners who assisted the board and supported it through all the legal twists and turns.

Without the ability to park a car at HCR, the value of owning an apartment, as well as the property's ability to attract vacationing guests, would have been severely reduced. The resort survived a serious threat. Nature, too, has menaced HCR, as we shall see in chapter 10.

Chapter 9
Talk Story—Coming Together

It is the annual dinner for owners and staff. People congregate by the pool. Above the western ridges, the sunset paints the clouds orange and pink and bronze. There is barbecue in the air and also baba ghanoush. People mingle and talk. One topic seems to be of predominant interest this evening: "How did you end up here? How did you become an owner? Why do you work here?" The answers reveal the wiles that HCR uses to captivate its people.

Everyone at HCR must, of course, first discover HCR. This discovery, in itself, may be through a stroke of luck. As reported by one guest,

> This is the first time here at the north end. We came by this lodge quite by accident and without reservations and late in the afternoon. Whoa! How fortunate for us because this place was exactly what we were looking for to finish out our stay—oceanfront paradise.

These fortunate first-time guests have often become repeat guests and even owners. Many paths have led to this discovery of HCR. In some cases, the path was short and led straight to HCR. In other cases, it twisted and turned a bit before it got here. Let's explore some of the passages that have brought people to HCR.

No Intent to Settle

From its earliest days, HCR has employed all the tricks in its bag to lure and capture its people. Often folks ended up at HCR without deliberately intending to arrive here. In several cases, people came to HCR without actually seeing their new home. At least, they went way down the road without seeing what was at the end of that road.

Mary McGregor and Dave Ballard
Mary McGregor was the first owner at HCR. For Mary, HCR's spell was cast long before it even existed. The place where HCR would later rise needed nothing more than its natural attractions and the charm of its people. Mary McGregor and her husband, David Ballard, had often visited Maui, but for one trip they were seeking a little solitude in a place where they did not know anyone. So in the early 1960s they came to Kaua'i. They stopped in Hanalei, where they met Auntie Louise. The rest is history. "Louise has been our friend forever. She's been many times in my house in Seattle," says Mary. Auntie Louise introduced Mary and Dave to many of the local residents, so they ended up with a broad circle of friends on the north shore. She also showed them around the north shore and took them fishing at several places, including Kepuhi Point. Following this personal introduction to the local culture and scenery, Mary and Dave returned frequently. Whenever they would come to the island, they would rent a room somewhere and drive up to Kepuhi Point. They bought a Volkswagen camper and kept it at the airport when they were not here. "We didn't sleep in it," Mary says. "We'd have a house, but we'd come over here and spend the day. When we first came, there was nothing here. But the Nishimotos kept the area nice."

Mary and Dave came to love this part of the island because of the relationships they built up with the Hawaiian people who lived here. They even acquired a few pieces of property in the area. So when HCR was being built, Mary and Dave were primed to buy in. They bought the first apartment sold (A-2). This was in 1967. One story suggests that the exact placement of the A building was modified at Mary's request. "We were the first ones there," recalls Mary. Later, when she retired, Mary moved full time to HCR.

Marion Burns

The spirit of HCR also began scheming for Marion Burns well before its body was constructed. Marion had a dear friend who had come to Kaua'i to teach at the middle school in Hanalei. This friend then met Jack Nishimoto, who was also a teacher, and later the principal, at the middle school. So when Marion and her husband first visited Kaua'i from California in the 1950s, they of course visited with their friends and, through them, met the Nishimotos, who were living in their house at Kepuhi Beach on land adjacent to the property that later became HCR. This connection is a deep link between the history of HCR and that of the north shore. The Nishimoto family, of course, were the previous owners of the land where HCR was built. The Nishimotos, in turn, had received the land in the dissolution of the Wainiha Hui. Marion recalls that first visit:

> We came and it was the first time we met each other, and it's like we had known each other for years. It was just like people who sit around the coffee table and talk about things. We talked about health care, and the school system, and problems with the church, just homely little problems. The same problems that we were talking about in California around our kitchen table, Jack and Ivy were talking about way out there. An interesting bit of sociology.

Marion and her husband traveled often to Kaua'i, and one time they noticed on Jack and Ivy's property a sign for a condo development to be built there. It was the Ha'i O Kauai Cottage Colony. "So when we went back to Honolulu," she says, "we went to the contractor. They had a map. We bought our condo, G-4, off this map. I think we signed up for one in '67. Several had already been sold by that time, too." So the Burnses bought not only sight unseen, but site unbuilt.

Averil and Howard Koch

Some paths to HCR were long.

It was dark. Close to midnight. The ship's captain called all hands out of the sack and onto the deck. "OK, guys," he said, "this is your first sight of US territory, and I thought you would like to see it." It was the sweeping beacon of Kilauea Lighthouse. It was the late '50s, and it was Howard Koch's first sight of Kaua'i, on a troop ship returning from the Korean conflict. Howard reminisces, "To this day, when we go to the lighthouse…" His voice trails off. "We were separated for almost a year and a half by the Korean War. We had just recently been married and now we've been married sixty-three years." And Averil remembers Howard down on the beach saying, "I never ever thought I would have a piece of property here, even after I saw the lighthouse. All those years!"

From HCR, you can see the Kilauea light sweeping above Princeville across the bay, the same light Howard saw from the ship—his first glimpse of home, his first glimpse of his home away from home.

Howard and Averil did not actually buy into HCR, or even see it again, until the early 1970s. They were in California, celebrating their marriage month with two other couples who happened to have been to HCR and wanted to buy a place there. They described it so enthusiastically that, after a largish Trader Vic's special adult beverage, Averil and Howard were convinced that they, too, wanted a place at HCR. They even tried to get on the midnight flight to Honolulu, only to discover that there was no midnight flight to Honolulu. Eventually, in the mid-1970s, they all made the trip and bought a unit. Eventually, Averil and Howard bought out their partners. They continue to blame their purchase on Trader Vic's.

This was a case of "love at first hearing." But love at first sight has frequently been the force that has moved people to become HCR owners. Often that love at first sight also sparked some spontaneous decision making.

Bob Eckert

Bob Eckert bought his unit during an interisland flight stopover at the Honolulu Airport. He recalls:

My first visit to Kaua'i and to HCR was in July 1976. I discovered Hanalei Colony Resort, but I was staying elsewhere. I had only one day up here. I drove up, saw Hanalei Colony Resort, and had lunch at the Anchorage. I went to the end of the road and went back a changed person because I had discovered I loved the north shore. I wasn't looking to buy. I didn't own any real estate; I was still renting an apartment in Geneva. I became a homeowner at HCR in 1984. I came as a guest for three days. I was planning to buy real estate, but I was planning to spend a week on the Big Island because the prices there were more in my range. But the three days staying here convinced me that this was the place.

What happened was this: On my last day, I called the owner of the unit where I was staying, who was the original owner and also a real estate broker. She called me back the next day and said, "We've talked to our accountant about selling, and he suggested that because of the tax consequences it was better to sell it on an installment sale rather than with a mortgage. Would that interest you?" I said, "Yes," and she said, "Well, you're going to have to sign some papers, and you're going to have to come to Oahu." And I said, "Well, fortunately, I'm stopping over in Oahu on my way to the Big Island."

When my plane landed in Oahu, I asked the flight attendant if I could get off the plane, and she said, "We don't normally let people." But I said, "It's really very important. I have to get something." She agreed to let me hop off for a few minutes. So I ran out, signed the paper, handed the seller a check, and ran back onto the plane. The attendant said, "Well, what kind of souvenir did you buy?" I said, "A condominium at Hanalei Colony

Resort." The rest of the paperwork was done by mail back in California. But yes, literally, I bought it on a stopover.

Dick Moody

Dick Moody's history with HCR goes way, way back, before there was an HCR. So it is appropriate that he should have an intriguing story about settling in to unit I-4. It shows just how HCR can beguile you into a spontaneous decision and then supply just a little bit of luck to move you along. Dick just happened to make a crucial telephone call at exactly the right minute.

Dick and his wife, Martha, were very familiar with HCR, since they had been coming to the north shore for many years, primarily for surfing. Early on, they stayed on the south shore or the east side, but after HCR was built, they stayed at the resort because it was close to the surf spots and was cheap, and units were always available. Part of the attraction of HCR was its convenience as a place to store clothes. "He got tired of packing. He was very spontaneous," recalls his daughter, Linda Stoskopf. "He just wanted to get on the airplane and go." Over the years, Dick became fascinated by unit I-4. He explains:

> For years and years and years, I-4 had never been occupied, not once in all those years. Every trip I kept looking at it, and I thought the view would be primo. The unit was all locked up, just locked up. Nobody was making any efforts to do anything to the building. The Colony didn't use it, didn't work on it, and had no incentive apparently to put it in their rental market. I originally decided to do something about it when I was home in Sunset Beach, California. I was in the Bank of America branch there, and it struck me that I had enough money in my pocket to see if I could do something about buying I-4. So I just picked up the phone in the bank and called Bank of America in Princeville and said, "I want to talk to the brokers in the bank."

I got on with a lady broker and told her I was interested in a unit at Hanalei Colony Resort, I-4. I asked her to research it and find out what's going on with it. And she said, "Well, that's strange, there are two men here asking about it." I asked the agent to tell me the story about that place. She said, "We're searching the title for it and we found the owners." I said, "Well, you know what, I want to make the owner an offer." I was in the Bank of America at home, and she was in the Bank of America in Princeville. I don't recall my offer, but I said, "I'll give you a $20,000 deposit on the chance that we could close it." She wrote up the offer while we were on the phone. These other two guys were sitting there when she wrote up my offer. They hadn't decided on buying anyways; they were just talking about it. I put a $20,000 deposit on it, subject to looking at it.

So I came home and I think the next week Martha and I jumped in an airplane and came over and finalized the deal. The unit was a mess. But I looked at it, and I loved the view. Martha thought it was awful. I wanted it, and it didn't matter that it was a mess. The location was the whole thing. I can see way down the coastline; I can see the whole, whole thing there.

State land records apparently were not able to help Dick identify the owner who sold him his unit. "I never really understood who owned I-4. It is supposed to have been a Hawaiian princess, and escrow said, 'Well, they were Hawaiian.' But perhaps not the princess part," Dick says laughing.

I've often wondered what would have happened if Dick had waited an hour to make his call to Princeville. Another interesting question: Who were those two guys?

Carol and Jim Thompson

HCR may be a dream for many, but for Carol Thompson, it began as the study of dreams. She first came to HCR around 1989 to participate in an Antioch College master's degree seminar on studying dreams. "You go to sleep in Hawai'i and you wake up in the morning and write down your dreams. The seminar group then helps you interpret them." What could be a more fitting activity for HCR than dreaming? Jim had been invited to come along on that trip but declined. "I'm tired of fourteen-story hotels on beaches," he recalls saying. "Carol called me and said, 'You made a big mistake. This is the closest thing to Tahiti that you will ever find under an American flag.'" She convinced Jim to accompany her to the seminar the next year, and they returned every year after for more than ten years. In 2000, they "put a realtor on patrol" to find them a unit at HCR, particularly in H building. They always stayed in the H building because they "like the centralness of it, and the flow, and the waving at everybody. When people want to visit, they look and see if we are at home." The spell of HCR had finally taken hold, because within a week, the realtor informed them that H-1 was available. They bought it.

Cissie Meyer

There is one person who can claim to have followed a path with perhaps the most twists and turns on the way to HCR. And she may have the record for the most miles traveled on her way here. A young girl first saw Hawai'i while passing through on the way from Singapore to Scotland. Royce Meyer's father was an oil engineer, so the family moved a lot. On that stop, Cissie—as she is universally known—attended a Leon Russell concert at the Shell in Oahu. She met someone from Taylor Camp and got the address of someone on Kaua'i. Later, she came back from Scotland to Hawai'i to go to college on Oahu and took a trip to Kaua'i to hike the Kalalau Trail. She then traveled to visit her father, who was in Norway. Next, she moved to Oahu to live on the north shore for a year but continued to travel back and forth to Kaua'i, spending the summer months and later a full year in Kalalau. In the mid-1970s, Cissie moved to Kauaʻi permanently, and in the early 1980s, she began working at HCR in housekeeping. Then she went up and worked at the Hanalei Bay Resort. She also worked as a boat tour guide on the side, where Rick Roderick, the HCR general manager, recruited her back to HCR to work at the front desk because, as he said, "We need some young people working down there," and because she was living nearby in Haʻena. She has, indeed, followed that twisting north shore road to HCR, a free and beautiful road. Cissie's spirit will be here forever—forever lovely and young.

These stories show that people have often arrived at HCR with no intent to settle here, or even to settle on Kauaʻi. But HCR's spell captured them. And luck played a role. For others, the discovery of HCR was the result of a deliberate search for property, or for a place, or for…something. Even for these, the spell of HCR, once cast, quickly put an end to any searching.

Seeking

People have come to HCR seeking many things that may be hard to define: peace, solitude, fun, or companionship. Sometimes they come looking for very specific things: property, work, or…surf.

Claire and Dusty Walker

Claire and Dusty Walker bought two units, D-3 and D-4, sight unseen. They were living on Oahu and had visited Kauaʻi, but they had never stayed at the resort or even come out to the end of the road that much. Their realtor told them, "I have these great properties at Hanalei. We really can get them for such a good price; you have to go see it." On the recommendation of the realtor, Claire and Dusty went ahead with the purchase. Claire recalls:

> Before the closing, we came with her to see it. We arrived at night, and it was pitch dark, and, of course, the next morning we wake up to this glorious view. We were sure

> then that we wanted to go ahead with it. We do want it. And when we first saw it we thought, *Oh yeah, that's perfect. It's on the ocean, it's exactly what we want.*

This was in 1973, and they purchased the leaseholds, which were later converted to fee simple. This was one of the short paths to HCR.

Dennie and Tom Stansell
A realtor was also responsible for bringing HCR to the attention of Dennie and Tom Stansell. This was a friend in California who represented the owner, Marion Burns. Tom said, "Why don't you go check it out?" So Dennie paid her first visit to the resort by herself, with the intent of checking out HCR. This was also the first time she or Tom had come to Kaua'i. Dennie remembers:

> When I came to the double bridge, and it's like the road was getting narrower and narrower, it's getting dark and I'm thinking, *That's not even going to hold the weight of a car. It's going to get down to a squirrel track. Where the hell am I going?* I got to HCR at night. The next morning it was just beautiful, and I loved it. I was in the C building and feeling a little more secure. I went back home and said, "We're buying it." We did make an offer on the unit I saw, and the sellers took it off the market. But then our current unit came onto the market and we made an offer and bought it.

Dennie had not seen the suite they purchased, and the first time Tom came over to HCR was the next summer. So this counts as a case of partial "sight unseen" commitment.

Laura and Tommy Richards
The future Laura Richards also came to HCR sight unseen. It was not property she was seeking, but lifestyle and work. She had been

living in Arkansas, and on the wall of her house was a picture of a tropical island. She did not particularly know where it was. One day she looked at the picture and said to her husband, "Let's go live in Hawai'i."

He said, "I'll ask you that again in a month." He did. Laura got a job at the Sheraton hotel in Princeville and they did come to Hawai'i, and, eventually, to HCR. They later discovered that the picture on the wall in Arkansas was a view of Ha'ena from Makana. It was Bali Hai calling to them across the sea.

Surfing brought Tommy Richards to Kaua'i. HCR's own charms eventually did the rest. Tommy's father was in the navy. While stationed on Oahu, he made balsa surfboards for his whole family. In the early 1960s, the family visited a friend on Kaua'i, stayed in a house on the north shore, and "got to surf Hanalei Bay with hardly anyone else," says Tommy. Later, in the mid-1970s, while living in California's San Fernando Valley, Tommy became "tired of surfing with four hundred guys that I did not know and having to wear a wet suit." So he decided, "'I am going home,' and I moved back here with a box of toothpaste and two surfboards."

But HCR's spell was not yet complete. Tommy later returned to the mainland. Finally, in the late 1990s, he visited the island again and met Laura. Fittingly, they met at HCR—in the office. That completed the spell. He soon began working at HCR. He and Laura married in 2001 and built a house in Wainiha.

Joe and Heather Shannon

Joe was a professional snowboarder. On a trip to New Zealand he met Heather, who was a professional surfer. Heather's endless summer joined up with Joe's endless winter. Together they passed nine winters in a row in four and a half years by traveling back and forth between the United States and New Zealand. They came to Kaua'i on a seven-month working holiday. When they became pregnant with their daughter Arlo, they sought real endless summer and found it on Kaua'i where the position of Resident Manager at HCR became available. "It played out perfectly. Now it's year-round summer all the time. It's a great place to raise a family," says Joe happily. Arlo, now a year old, agreed with a smile. So, once again, a little searching aided by a little luck brought this family to HCR.

Like Attracts Like

Oftentimes, HCR will deploy existing owners as bait to lure future owners. People have often arrived at HCR initially as guests of owners and have then become owners themselves.

Pat Montague

In Honolulu, Pat and Morgan Montague were friends with Tom Moffatt, who was one of the original owners. The Montagues occasionally visited HCR as guests of Moffatt, eventually became partners in the unit, and finally bought out Moffatt's share. Pat remembers her first visit to HCR in 1971, only two years after it was built:

> It was terrible weather. My daughter was five years old then, so it was kind of hard to entertain her. All I did was cook. These places were built without windows. The kitchens were more closed in, so it was kind of uncomfortable. I don't think they had the swimming pool. And we couldn't have used it because it was pretty cold. So that's the first time.

A less than promising introduction, to be sure, but they were ensnared by HCR anyway.

Aggie and Roger Parlee

Claire and Dusty Walker were responsible for luring Roger and Aggie Parlee. They were friends in Honolulu, and the Parlees visited the Walkers at HCR. "There was no thought," said Aggie. "We just bought in with them. It was just our friends and the ambiance of the place."

Nancee and Rich Sells

The Walkers were also instrumental in hooking Nancee and Rich Sells. The Sells also came across HCR while deliberately looking to buy a place on Kaua'i and were specifically looking at HCR. They came to HCR in 1975 looking for a place, having flown in from Japan. This was their first visit to Kaua'i, and they stayed at HCR. Rich remembers:

> We knew right away that we wanted to become owners. We stayed in Po'ipu first. It was OK. Then we came up here and saw this and we said, "Oh, this is really nice." We had seen it advertised in a magazine. We had the reservations already before we came.

Rich recalls meeting Dusty and Claire Walker, with whom they eventually partnered. Rich says:

> I went into the office, and there was this tall, white-haired guy who walked in there with a cup of coffee. Anyway, we asked the people at the front desk, we said, "Are any of these places for sale?" And she says, "Well, we don't really do anything about that. You'll have to see a realtor." When I was walking out, this white-haired guy said, "Hey, come here. I want to talk to you." It was Dusty Walker, and he said, "We're looking for a partner." And I said, "Well, that might even be a better way to get into the deal." So we went up to D-4 and met Claire and sat and talked, and they explained that they had two partners and both these guys needed to be bought out. I said, "Well, I'll buy the one." So we made a deal and I bought his third. It was simply a matter of heart over mind. We liked it so much that we just decided to jump, and we said if we make a mistake, this could be the worst mistake. Our friends

all thought we were crazy. It was all of $13,000. But we jumped, and Claire and Dusty became fast friends.

Nancee Sells describes how the spirit of HCR can be compelling:

> As a young couple, we used to say to each other, "We don't ever want to be tied to any place where we feel like we have to go back every year." Until we came here and saw this place, and we fell head over heels. Nor did we ever feel like we *had* to come, but we *wanted* to come.

Georgia Henry

The Walkers and the Sells then teamed up to lure Georgia Henry. Georgia first came to HCR in 1979 as a guest of her friend Claire Walker. "I went for a little vacation, and I never left," says Georgia. In response to a request from the Walkers and the Sells, Georgia became manager of HCR around 1981. This was not a far-fetched idea, since by then Georgia was working as the executive secretary for the general manager of the Kaua'i Surf Hotel, now the Marriott. Georgia remained as HCR manager through 1986 and has continued to visit ever since.

The Final Resort

Many people ended up at HCR after experiencing the other Islands or other parts of Kaua'i. It may have taken them a bit longer to discover HCR, but once they found it, it conjured its magic spell. And the ritual of love at first sight still worked.

Barbara and Bob Johnstone

For a number of years, Bob and Barbara Johnstone would come to Kaua'i and stay at the Grand Hyatt in Po'ipu. In 1999, on his way back from dropping Barbara and their son Ryan off to hike the Kalalau Trail, Bob noticed HCR for the first time. "I pulled into the parking lot, went to the office, got a brochure, looked around, and I thought, *This is really cool. Let's stay here the next time.*" Back in town, Bob had lunch and went to a realtor. "I lived in Oahu in the 1960s, and I really learned to love Hawai'i. What's for sale?" The realtor offered Bob several houses at a million dollars, but this was not what he was thinking about. Then the realtor mentioned that an apartment was available for sale at HCR, unit L-4. But L-4 was rented, and Bob could not get in to see it. Instead, "I saw M-3, which was available for viewing. Thought this was totally cool." Barbara and Ryan agreed. "We went into town, had dinner, came back, walked the beach, and made an offer the next day."

They had had no intention of buying a place on that trip. The sellers proposed a "ridiculous" counteroffer, which the Johnstones declined. They continued their visit to the other Islands and returned home. But HCR nagged at them. So Bob made a final offer, which the sellers accepted. "And that was that." They had seen unit M-3, but they bought unit L-4. They never saw the suite they bought "until escrow closed, and we came over in 2000 and spent our first vacation here. We had no idea what the view was like and when we first went out on the lanai Barbara started hyperventilating because the view is pretty good!"

So, in another case of property blindness, they had spontaneously purchased a place they had not seen. Surely this is evidence that HCR exercises a compelling allure over us, its people!

Lionel Medeiros and Mary Neudorffer

Lionel Medeiros and Mary Neudorffer had been visiting Kaua'i and the north shore for many years, usually staying in Hanalei, and had noticed HCR on their way to Tunnels and Ke'e. One time they stopped to investigate the grounds, and then on a subsequent trip to the Islands Lionel thought, "*Gee, try something different.*" So they stayed at HCR and "really enjoyed it." Then later, when Lionel was looking for property on Kaua'i, he explored several units at HCR and settled on unit B-4. About a year later, Mary also bought an apartment at the resort. The spell can be very powerful!

Moreen and Chuck Williams

Moreen and Chuck Williams visited Kaua'i several times and started out staying on the south shore. But they always visited the north shore and found that they preferred it. So they stayed in various hotels on the north shore and eventually found HCR. After that, they returned almost every year. Even when HCR was closed while it was being rebuilt after Iniki, they rented a house close to the resort. They were so committed to HCR and their family had such memorable experiences that it was their children who bought into HCR.

Molly and George Ksander

Molly and I had a similar experience. We had often visited the other Islands but we first visited Kaua'i after Iniki with the thought of helping to support its revival. As most people do, we visited the north shore. "Got up to the north shore and fell in love," Molly says. She was especially enchanted by the descent into Hanalei Valley. So for our next trip we scoured guidebooks for places to stay on the north shore, and HCR sounded unbeatable. It was. That first time on the north shore, we stayed at HCR. Later, after staying in many places from Hanalei to Ha'ena, we decided to buy our own property as a base for family events and to provide a deeper sense of belonging to this area we had learned to love. We spent some time researching and visiting several properties in Wainiha and Ha'ena, but none were just right. When a unit at HCR became available, we viewed it, drove into Hanalei, and "after a prolonged reflective moment" at the Wishing Well Shave Ice truck, we bought it that afternoon. Fortunately the truck was open that day. That moment of reflection has made me wonder whether HCR is like the sweetness of macadamia nut ice cream hidden in the mango, banana, papaya, passion fruit shave ice that is the north shore of Kaua'i.

Heather Halpern and John Brekke

John Brekke and Heather Halpern were familiar with Kaua'i and used to bring their kids over, staying in rental properties all across the island. They finally decided that they wanted to buy their own place. Their realtor showed them a number of options, but none were appealing. "Until, one day, the agent said, 'Look, you didn't like Princeville. Well, there's one more place you might want to see.' We came here and went, 'Oh, man.' And then, we met a guest in unit C-3 on the beach, and they let us in and we looked and we went, 'This is it. Love at first sight.'" They immediately plugged into the HCR community.

Jody and Carl Woodbury

It only took one visit to convince Carl and Jody Woodbury that they wanted to be part of HCR. They had previously gone to Maui, but, as Carl recalls:

> It got too crowded for us. So, we thought we'd try Kaua'i and HCR. And walked into this very unit, actually, first time we were here. We stayed for two weeks that time, and I went up to the front office to reserve the exact same unit a year ahead of time, offered to pay the full amount right on the spot because I fell in love with this unit. And the office staff told me, "No, that's not how it works." So I reserved three weeks for the next year, premium oceanfront, but I couldn't get G-2. And then she said, as I was going out the door, "By the way, it's for sale." So that started the process.

Like so many others, they had tried the rest of the Islands before committing to Kaua'i and HCR as the best.

Onto the Generations

Given the family-oriented nature of HCR, it is not surprising that it is populated by a number of multigenerational families. Owners bring their children. The kids then begin visiting on their own. Then they bring the grandchildren. The younger generation may inherit the family apartment or acquire their own. The spell of HCR gets into their genes.

Alicia Cortrite

Alicia Cortrite is grateful to her mother for starting this cycle in their family. Her mother and her husband traveled frequently to the Far East and were looking for a stopping point in between so the trip would not be so long. According to Alicia, they fell in love with HCR. When unit J-1 became available, they decided to buy it. "It was one of those things that they just fell into. They certainly weren't looking for someplace to stay on Kaua'i. They loved the island. They always would go to out-of-the-way places. HCR would be the sort of place that we ended up."

Linda and Darrel Stoskopf

Linda and Darrel Stoskopf came to HCR through Linda's dad, Dick Moody. But Linda did not even know about HCR for a good long time after her mother and father arrived there. She and her siblings just thought their parents were going to Honolulu. It was "ten years before they shared with myself and my brother and sister that they owned a unit in Hawai'i," Linda says. She recalls:

> It was truly their getaway. In our minds, they were always going to Honolulu. My mom was always cooking at the condo and she wanted some pampering. So they always stopped in Oahu before they came home.

Linda's first experience of HCR did not start well. Her dad's apartment, I-4, was rented, so they were put in a different building. "We got there at night, and there was no one in the office, and we probably did not even know that there was a resident manager. Our first impression was, 'Oh, great! What kind of a place did Dad buy? The water heater doesn't work.'" But the heater was fixed the next day, and they soon moved into her dad's suite.

After Linda's mother passed, Dick asked "if we three kids would like to have a second condominium at HCR. So, not being complete fools, we said, 'Oh, we would love to have it, Dad.' So that is how he bought H-3." This unit was bought sight unseen and with a bit of luck. One day in the late 1990s, Dick called a real estate company to ask what was available. The agent told him that one of the first-floor units in D building was available. But while the agent was discussing the D unit on the phone, another agent at the next desk said that she had just gotten a call from the owner of H-3, who wanted to sell. Dick thought that would be a better choice, so he made the deal then and there. It was Dick's telephone luck coming through once again.

"Thrilled!" laughs Linda, recalling her reaction to her first sight of her new apartment. "My sister and I were thrilled to have a second unit there, because we do things together as a family. And we liked the view."

Owen Paepke

Owen Paepke's family first began visiting Kaua'i in the early 1970s. They had visited other Islands, but Kaua'i quickly became their favorite. On one trip, they rented a house near Tunnels. The house seemed "quite elaborate, with a baby grand piano and china, not what you would call an imperative," chuckles Owen. "They became aware of HCR, and this seemed to be more appropriate for a beach vacation, so from then on they stayed at HCR." Then shortly after Iniki, "The folks went over there and next I knew they owned a unit." After that, Owen would not let has dad take his checkbook on vacations, because "who knew what might happen?" They used the HCR apartment as a frequent getaway spot. In the course of time, Owen inherited the unit and continues the tradition.

HCR's spells are for the generations.

It may take more time or less, it may operate impulsively, and it may require a bit of luck, but what all these stories show is the power of the spell that HCR casts over its people—the attraction it exercises that lures folks to discover HCR in the first place and then compels them to return again and again.

So how did you get here? Who—or what—lured you? How were you ensnared by HCR's magic spell?

Chapter 10

Peril in Paradise

As of this writing, HCR has existed for more than forty-five years. It has changed over time, in small ways and large. It has evolved to meet the changing needs and wishes of its owners and guests. It has become part of the local community. It appears to be a secure and permanent institution. It is in a special place, with a wonderful climate and magnificent views. "The most beautiful meeting of mountains and ocean," as Bob Eckert pictures it. Yet HCR has been severely threatened and, at times, almost destroyed. And the threats exist even now. The very charms that help make HCR so special—its topography and its climate—also pose serious threats to its continued existence.

Volcanic action built the island; it piled up layer after layer of lava from the sea floor to the top of the island. Then came the trade winds and the rain, which eroded the island into the ridges and valleys and dunes that give shape to the land. Then came the tsunamis and floods and hurricanes to fine-tune how—and where—we live with the land and the sea. The things that so attract people to HCR, its location, geology, and climate, are simultaneously the things that put HCR at risk. Any number of times, in many ways, HCR could have been destroyed. It should not be taken for granted. There is peril in paradise.

Unfriendly Water

The presence of a gate on the highway before the descent into Hanalei Valley is warning enough that nature may demand our attention and inconvenience us from time to time. Many of us have been in the Princeville food market when word went around that the gate would be closing due to rising tides and heavy rain runoff. We quickly finished shopping and headed home to beat the rising rivers. Indeed, we have seen firsthand that the name *Wainiha* means "angry, hostile, or unfriendly water," presumably in reference to its floods and storm tides. The archives of the *Garden Island* are full of stories about extreme high tides, rising rivers, and flash floods. So it is not surprising that storm-driven floods have had an impact on HCR.

Darrel Stoskopf recalls "those stressful moments when we had flight schedules and then discovered that the road was closed due to flooding." Several owners have stories of waves breaking across the beach and rolling underneath HCR buildings into the grassy courtyard. Storm surge often washes giant driftwood tree trunks up HCR's streambed, even beyond the footbridge. In 1983, Georgia Henry, manager at the time, reported that "high tide with thirty-foot waves brought sea water under F and G buildings all the way to the barbecue area, killing plants, filling the stream with sand, and ruining some carpets. The sand was removed from the stream bed, but two days later heavy surf again filled the stream with sand." Moreen and Chuck Williams recall a storm "where the water actually came up over the highway and it was kind of scary." Even in normal weather, the rip current on Kepuhi Beach is dangerous. In May 2010, the *Garden Island* reported two instances in which rescue tubes located at HCR by the Hanalei Rotary Club saved lives.

Floods do not only come from the sea. They can come also from the land when there is heavy rain. Darrel Stoskopf remembers a storm with wind and rain so heavy that "I thought it was going to break the window. We got out of bed because I was worried the window was going to crater."

Peril in Paradise | 157

Storm surge in HCR's stream has swept past the footbridge toward maintenance and recreation areas and has overtopped the stream banks, November 1989. Bridge rail is visible at lower left, and driveway can be seen at upper left. (Courtesy HCR Archives)

The "great flood" of March 2012 shows how storm-driven wind, rain, and tides can seriously impact life around HCR. Kaua'i experienced almost a week of extreme rain and winds. The *Garden Island* reported that there were high-wind advisories, high-surf warnings, and continuous rain. Wainiha and Ha'ena experienced close to thirty-two inches of rain in twenty-four hours. At one point, the Hanalei River rose six feet within ninety minutes. A landslide at Waikoko blocked Kuhio Highway, and a fallen tree near Lumaha'i prevented travel from the HCR area to Hanalei. Laura Richards reported more than forty landslides. A falling tree knocked out all power to HCR for almost three days. Extreme wind blew water into some units. Plumbing throughout Ha'ena was backed up and flooded the streets. People could not leave Wainiha for three days. As a result, neighbors and staff began staying in rooms at HCR. Stranded guests were accommodated at a reduced rate.

The *Garden Island* reported that the Mediterranean Gourmet opened in the middle of the storm with "only four employees and no electricity. For two days in a row, the restaurant donated food to guests and owners of the nearby Hanalei Colony Resort." Tommy Richards recalls that "luckily we had a lot of food at home in our freezer, so we just kind of brought it to the grill and fed people who could not go anywhere and did not have any groceries." Resort staff who lived in the area prepared food at home and brought it to HCR to help feed the guests. "I didn't have power at my house for probably twenty-four to thirty-six hours," said Debra Jason, Laura Richards's assistant. "I ended up staying at Laura's house because she had power over there. Well, my place also got flooded, so that was another reason to stay at Laura's." Tommy Richards sees a silver lining in the cloud of such unsettling events:

> It is really satisfying when we do have a little disaster that we help our guests understand that this is something that most people do not get to see, the real aloha spirit of our 'ohana at the resort. Everybody takes care of you, just like you are part of our family.

This flooding was caused by weather that was only slightly more extreme than normal. Imagine the impact of rare conditions that dramatically exceed these normal variations.

Higher Than the Trees

The Hawaiian Islands have always been subject to tsunamis. Before contact and after, whole valleys have been depopulated and landscapes altered. Tsunamis are caused by great earthquakes in the ocean or at its edge. Large pieces of the sea floor suddenly sink or rise, and this movement creates large waves in the ocean. These waves can travel thousands of miles at five hundred to six hundred miles per hour. When the waves hit land, they can be very high—over one hundred feet—and extremely destructive. The US Geological Survey (USGS) reports that Kaua'i has experienced a damaging tsunami once every twelve years since 1868. In 1946, and again in 1957, Wainiha and Ha'ena suffered major tsunamis, which shaped their appearance and their population. Events have also occurred that were less destructive but still stand out in the memories of the HCR community and its neighbors.

On April 1, 1946, a large earthquake (magnitude 8.1 according to the USGS) occurred in the Aleutian Islands. The first tsunami waves hit Kaua'i early in the morning. There was no warning. Wainiha and Ha'ena were badly hurt. At Wainiha, the highest wave was estimated at twenty-four feet above sea level; at Ha'ena it was forty-five feet. At least fourteen people died on Kaua'i.

The *Honolulu Star Bulletin* reported that "all bridges at Wainiha…were washed out…The tiny village of Wainiha is flat. The Nakatsuji store and the surrounding houses took the full force of the wave." Two houses were washed more than three hundred feet from their foundations. At Ha'ena, nine houses and the YMCA Camp Naue were destroyed. A fortunate coincidence allowed supplies to be brought into Ha'ena and casualties to be taken out. "When the Waikoko Stream bridge…was washed out by the second big wave, a county truck was stranded on the Ha'ena side of the stream…By placing planks over the wrecked Waikoko stream, supplies were carried across to the truck and from there delivered to Wainiha and carried into Ha'ena."

A few days later, the *Honolulu Star Bulletin* provided more details on the "heroism, courage, and faith in God in the face of disaster and isolation." It reported that the Mormon Chapel on the beach at Ha'ena was destroyed, with the loss of eight lives from the small population of sixty residents.

> The [tsunami] hit in four waves. The first roused the villagers so that the majority immediately sought escape. Some time then elapsed before the three large waves overwhelmed the summer houses, the permanent residents, and Camp Naue.

The article tells a tale of tragedy and heroism. Nine adults and seventeen children took refuge in the Mormon church. One of the adults present, a local man, Hilario Aquino, recounted his tale to the *Star Bulletin*, which reported that when the waves hit the church, [Aquino] was tossed out among the children. He swam about rescuing the children and lifting them up into the large trees of the church yard. When the waves subsided, ten of the children were safely clinging to the trees, and the parents all agreed that Mr. Aquino had saved their lives…The [second] wave lifted the roof off the church and with it, the people…Mr. Kalani said he assisted an injured woman up into the tree when the next wave hit. Most of the other adults had also climbed into the trees. When the last wave receded, leaving water waist high, the adults began hunting the children and taking them to safety.

David Laamea rushed on foot from the Hanalei firehouse, where he was going off duty, to Ha'ena, wading waist deep through streams and climbing hills. He found his wife with a broken leg, hanging desperately from a tree. He also found three of his nine children in the trees where Mr. Aquino had left them. He then received help in rescuing his family. Henry Gomes, a worker at the Wainiha Powerhouse, organized a volunteer rescue team. As this team descended the mountain, they saw Mr. Laamea and used a stretcher from the Ha'ena school to get his wife back up to the Powerhouse and eventually to the Kilauea dispensary. Mr. Laamea was not able to find three of his missing children. Jack Nishimoto was the first to reach Ha'ena village after wading through streams where the bridges were down. He found his home gone. Mrs. Lily Dorian witnessed the destruction of her neighbors' homes. She watched one home drift out to sea. Mrs. Hanohano, with her three-year-old daughter and Mrs. Hashimoto, rushed to the hills when the second wave, "higher than the trees," struck and carried them inland over brush and barbed wire. They held on to branches until the water receded. Mrs. Alice Alohikea, who at the time was more than sixty years of age, climbed into a kamani tree until the waters receded. In all, fifty-two of the residents survived. One of the long-term effects of the 1946 tsunami was the creation in 1949 of what is now the tsunami early warning system.

Another massive earthquake, magnitude 8.6 according to the USGS, occurred in the Aleutian Islands on March 9, 1957. On Kaua'i, damage from the 1957 tsunami was worse than that of 1946, but there were no deaths. The highest wave was thirty-four feet above sea level at Ha'ena and thirty-eight feet at Wainiha. This time there were early warnings. According to the *Honolulu Advertiser*, warnings were communicated widely. Ha'ena residents received telephone warnings from people in other places on Kaua'i. Those wanting to leave were taken out by helicopter. "Out of twenty-nine homes that once stood at Ha'ena, only four can now be lived in. A YMCA boys' camp, recently repaired from 1946 tidal wave damage, was washed out to sea." Mrs. Juliet Wichman provided shelter for about fifty Ha'ena refugees, who were eventually evacuated by helicopter to a shelter at the Hanalei School. She also organized a Red Cross shelter at her home in Ha'ena.

Hobey Goodale, Kaua'i resident and author, remembered those days in a 2011 *Garden Island* article:

> Wainiha had some damage to the Nakatsuji store, the bridge, and some of the *lo'i* [taro patch]…The bridge was out…Henry Gomez went up the road from Wainiha to where he stood for the 1946 wave, and this was not enough for the 1957 wave; he had to hug an electric pole or be swept away.

Goodale also recalled that a ferry system was set up to move people and supplies across the Wainiha Stream and that marines from the Pacific Missile Range Facility were using helicopters to bring in supplies. Eventually, a US Navy landing ship was used to bring in heavy equipment and supplies. It landed telephone poles, electrical equipment, trucks, and bulldozers on Ha'ena Beach. The captain would "come into the bay as close as he could to the reef on the Tunnels side, drop an anchor, and come right in and up the beach." Residents who lived on the flats near the Maniniholo dry cave were able to get their houses back on the foundations, reattached to the water and electricity services, so that "when the electricity was turned on they moved right back into their homes." But this was "not so [for] some of the newer houses nearer the beach. There was major damage and some of the owners never came back."

As we saw earlier, the 1957 tsunami set the stage for the creation of HCR when it swept away the old motel at Kepuhi Point. The *Garden Island* reported that according to Jack Nishimoto, the owner of the Hale Hoomaha Motel, the wave "just smashed everything. It carried the whole motel building about five hundred yards inland and across the road." Memories of the 1957 tsunami linger at HCR today. Bob Eckert tells the story he heard from one of our housekeepers who had been walking down the road holding hands with her brother and sister when she heard palm trees around them "popping" as they broke apart, followed by the sound of bubbles as the water trapped them. Pua Dorian, who was HCR's assistant manager and night manager in the 1970s, later told Tom Stansell how, as a little girl, she escaped the 1957 tsunami in the top of a palm tree.

On March 11, 2011, an earthquake with magnitude of 9.0 according to the USGS occurred just off the east coast of Japan at 7:46 p.m. Hawaiian Standard Time. This was one of the largest earthquakes ever recorded. It shifted portions of Japan almost nine feet closer to North America and actually affected the rotation of the earth. A portion of the sea floor near Japan was pushed vertically upward from fifteen to twenty-four feet, pushing a huge volume of water out of its way. Some of this water hit Japan in the form of a massive tsunami that measured up to 180 feet above normal in one location. Everything built on vast areas of land was destroyed, and, eventually, the nuclear plant at Fukushima failed disastrously. In all, tens of thousands of people were killed or injured. Tsunami waves caused some degree of damage throughout the Pacific Ocean region from Russia to South America and the islands of the South Pacific.

In Hawai'i, a tsunami warning was issued at approximately 9:30 p.m. On Kaua'i, residents and visitors responded by moving to high ground and public assembly centers. The *Garden Island* reported that

> approximately 4,500 visitors were evacuated from resorts and hotels…[and] roughly 2,300 people filtered into

holding areas…At the Hanalei Colony Resort…about 130 guests evacuated around 10:00 p.m. from the beachfront resort to Princeville or Kilauea. "Once the sirens went on, they pretty much made their way to their vehicles," said Concierge Juan Gomez. "We were expecting something big. We were scared," Gomez said. "Any warning is good enough excuse to get out."

John Brekke assisted in the tsunami response at HCR and recalls that day with emotion. He and Juan Gomez and resident manager Susan Emma "went around, got everybody out, locked all the doors, made sure everything was shut down." They got everyone out of their rooms safely by 11:00 p.m. and locked the place down. John remembers:

When we were pulling out, I just turned around and I stood there and I thought, *I wonder if this is going to be here tomorrow*, and drove off. So, that was a real sinking… you know? We slept all night in the Foodland parking lot. And of course, you can't really sleep because we're listening to the radio and we'd doze off. Everybody's in cars. Nobody was really partying. I mean, there was a seriousness about it.

According to the *Garden Island*, "The Pacific Tsunami Warning Center initially forecast a six-foot wave…with the potential to cause serious devastation to coastal areas. When it arrived in its weakened state just after 3:00 a.m., a modest bump in sea levels was recorded. Reports of six- to eight-foot waves…were received from Hanalei." The headline read, "Tsunami Leaves Kaua'i Mostly Unscathed." There was scattered damage around the island and debris in marinas. There were no injuries or deaths.

Most staff and guests returned to HCR between 8:00 and 10:30 a.m. the following day. "We are back now (8:00 a.m.) and all looks well," Brekke e-mailed. "Based on a visual inspection of the beach this morning, the surge was only slightly higher than normal high tide. The tide line was just at the reach of the vegetation on the beach, no threat to the structures at all," he later e-mailed. "Oh, man, when the final all-clear came, it was like…it was just an incredible relief. Driving back here, you have that sense of how fragile things are, but you're just so grateful that it's still there."

On October 27, 2012, at 5:04 p.m. Hawaiian Standard Time, a 7.7 magnitude earthquake followed by a 5.8 magnitude aftershock occurred in the Queen Charlotte Islands off Canada's western coast, according to the USGS. The *Garden Island* reported that a tsunami warning for Hawai'i was issued at 7:08 p.m., and residents of low-lying areas were told to evacuate to higher ground. Throughout the Islands, more than one hundred thousand people were evacuated to high ground. The evacuation was complete by 10:28 p.m., when the first waves were expected. The biggest waves, around six feet, were expected at Hanalei. In the event, the highest waves recorded in the Islands were about five feet at Maui. The wave at Hanalei was about six inches. No serious damage, injuries, or deaths were reported. HCR guests and staff evacuated according to standard procedure and were all back by 3:50 a.m. "We lived once again," said Laura Richards.

And in order to go on living through future tsunamis, the same preparations and evacuations will be carried out. This one could have been much worse. Sometimes you get lucky. Remember 1946 and 1957! You do not know in advance if a predicted event will be a disaster, so you respond to all predictions on the assumption that they might be. HCR lives on the edge, in more ways than one. *Ha'i o Kaua'i!*

A Strong and Piercing Wind

Kaua'i had been hit by hurricanes before 1992, notably Nina in 1957, Dot in 1959, and Iwa on November 23, 1982. Of these, Iwa (frigate bird) had the biggest impact on Kaua'i, but the amount of damage was nowhere near that caused by Iniki in 1992. It did not shut HCR down for very long. But Iwa left its own memories.

Iwa

Cissie Meyer was in the housekeeping department at the time and remembers living through Iwa:

> It was in '82. They said that there's a hurricane that's going to definitely hit the Islands. It's going to be a category 1. By the time it hit us, it was a category 2. Everyone took it very seriously and said category 2, that's a big hurricane. So, we evacuated the HCR guests, and then we went up to one of the stone houses where a friend of ours was living in Kilauea. They had a generator and everything, and so we had it pretty easy. But we went out in the eye and it was just like a starry night, and everything had started to be destroyed. But then, it came back. The eye went right over Kaua'i. Which means that the wind comes from one direction, then the eye is in the center and it clears, and it comes from the other direction. So, it hits you from both sides. I think it cleared in the middle of the night. The next morning everything was devastated. There was no water and electricity, and no one was really prepared at that time for that big of a hurricane. So, that was really traumatic on the whole island. We came back down, and I remember seeing Laura Check and Averil Koch and Laura Richards (Laura Beemer as she was at the time). What we basically did was take the trash out so that nothing would rot. We basically did some cleanup.

**Damage to roof of K building caused by hurricane Iwa in 1982.
(Courtesy HCR Archives)**

Iwa was "god-awful," recalls Georgia Henry, who was manager at that time. She explains:

> It was just horrible. It was fortunate that nobody lost their life there; it was some kind of miracle. The resort

itself suffered enormous damage. We had roofs lying in the creek and the backyard of L-2. We had no water or electricity for eight days, I think it was, so there was no way to cook anything. One of our owners had a huge freezer in his condo in H building. It was full of food because he owned a restaurant in California. It was two days before Thanksgiving and everybody had turkey, and hams, and what have you. It was a horrible, horrible time. We had to boil water for coffee out on that barbecue that we enjoyed then and now. That was our way of life for about eight days until they could truck some water in. We had to use the swimming pool for water in buckets to carry in and flush the toilets. I got everybody out, but there was somebody in F building, honeymooners, and they decided they were staying.

Apparently the romantic attraction of HCR trumps even hurricanes. Love does conquer all.

The resort was fully operational again in mid-December and was the only resort on the island with beachfront units. According to Laura Richards, "I think that was only shutting down buildings I, J, and K for a period of months." The damage was primarily to doors, windows, and roofs and was repaired by June 1983. The impact of Iniki would be very much more severe. It would threaten the continued existence of HCR.

Iniki

A tropical storm was benignly traveling west in the Pacific Ocean when it suddenly intensified into a category 4 hurricane and changed course to the north, directly toward Kaua'i. It was September 11, 1992, and the storm was Iniki (strong and piercing wind). Estimates of wind strength vary. Sustained winds from 145 to 160 mph or greater were reported, with gusts up to 175 mph. The navy's weather station on Makaha Ridge recorded gusts of 227 mph just before breaking down. According to the Weather Channel, "Iniki was the deadliest and by far the costliest hurricane to ever strike Hawai'i. The death toll of four was remarkably small for an intense hurricane. Adjusted for inflation, Iniki caused roughly $3 billion in damages. More than 14,000 homes were affected, with 1,421 destroyed and 5,152 with major damage." On Kaua'i, there was little loss of life but very extensive damage. While wind was the cause of most of the damages, storm surge and waves obliterated many structures along Kaua'i's southern shore. For HCR, Iniki was the worst of times. But it was also the best of times.

In the Eye of the Storm. Pat Montague had left HCR just before Iniki hit, but her husband, Morgan, had stopped in Honolulu to visit their friend Tom Moffatt. Pat remembers watching television at home in San Francisco and seeing her husband on the local evening news because he was one of those on the last plane out of Hawai'i before the storm.

Janne Hayward describes how she and Bill sort of "honeymooned" through Iniki:

> Bill Hayward and I got married in August of '92. And a story about him, he ran the San Francisco marathon and won in his age group the week after we got married. Two weeks after that, we came to Hawai'i because he was still on the board. And I was still the accountant. We had the board meeting in early September. Bill returned to San Francisco for work, and I stayed on to do some other work at HCR. I talked to him on a Thursday night. I was to come home on Friday, September 11th of 1992. He said, "You should be careful because there's a hurricane coming." Of course, I don't listen to the radio or have a laptop or anything out there. So I said, "Oh, yeah. I've been here before and I went through Iwa. So, whatever." He said, "No, no. It's a really big hurricane, and it's coming and it's going to hit Kaua'i." And indeed it did. We got up the next day when the sirens went off and evacuated everybody. I stayed with Jane Yadao, HCR's general manager at the time, at her house in Kilauea through the hurricane, and for just about a week before I could get home back to San Francisco.

Roger and Aggie Parlee were also staying at HCR when Iniki arrived. They were alerted by the tsunami alarm system, radio alerts, and HCR staff knocking on their door. About nine o'clock in the morning, they evacuated to Princeville along with Mary and Dee McGregor. They went first to the Princeville Hotel but encountered a long line there. So Roger went next door to the Hanalei Bay Resort and booked a condo for the four of them. Aggie recalls that "it was a horrifying experience to be up there, because tiles were flying all over. You could see them coming off the Princeville Hotel, and we had to stay in the basement all night." Afterward, they returned to HCR and stayed for two weeks to help with the initial cleanup. Aggie told Roger, "I don't ever want another candlelight dinner, because we didn't have any electricity for those two weeks."

In a late September letter, Howard Koch, president of the AOAO at that time, provided owners with a few details about the immediate reaction to the storm:

> Jane Yadao roused our guests and owners early in the morning on the day of the storm, informing them of the situation and directing them to safety according to our disaster plan. Jane and the staff taped the windows and took other steps to minimize damage. Laura and Peter Beemer, who were resident managers at the time, remained on the property throughout the storm, securing it as best they could. They were forced to move during the storm because L building was destroyed by flying objects such as lanai roofs. Fortunately, no one was injured.

On the day before the storm, Laura Richards (Laura Beemer at the time) with her husband, Peter Beemer, were hiking in Waimea Canyon, out of all contact, and when they emerged late in the day, they checked into the Waimea Plantation Cottages for the night. Very tired, they went immediately to sleep. In the middle of the night, they woke up to lightning and a raging sea. They turned on the TV to see what was happening and quickly caught up with events. They returned immediately to HCR to prepare for the coming storm. Laura and Peter and several friends holed up in unit H-1. They put the kids in the closet covered by pillows. They put two mattresses over end tables and climbed under them. Laura remembers that there were tornados in Wainiha Bay.

Dick Moody also remembers the immediate response to the storm:

> When Iniki came, they vacated everybody who lived on the peninsula out there. And Laura stayed back. She's the one who took care of what was left of the place. Laura earned her stars during Iniki, because everybody else left and she stayed there, and then she went around through the units and picked up things of value and stored them for the owners.

Cissie Meyer had vivid memories of living through Iniki:

> Then we heard that there was a really strong hurricane out there that was Iniki, but it was supposed to go beyond us. At the last minute in the middle of the night, it veered straight to Kaua'i. I had a friend call me in the middle of the night and say, "Cissie, I don't know if you're watching anything"—it was like eleven thirty at night. "But this hurricane's coming straight at us, and it's a category 5." We had already been through a category 2 and thought that was the end of the world. So we were all, "Oh, we're going to die."
>
> It was supposed to start coming in at noon the next day, and it was not supposed to hit us until like five in the afternoon. Well, everyone went out and did what they had to do, but Mayor JoAnn Yukimura said, "Everyone get where you have to go; I want the roads cleared." It was a daytime hurricane. That saved a lot of lives; it saved a lot of fires and things like that. They went up and down the streets with their megaphones saying, "Evacuate. Evacuate. Evacuate." They were really on it.

> So everyone evacuated, got to where they were going, but we were terrified, thinking, *Oh, it's just going to blow everything away.* And it pretty much did. But it was so eerie because the really gale force winds started at noon. And we thought we had a little bit longer; the branches were breaking as we were driving up to Princeville. It was already really, really scary in the early afternoon. So again, here came the hurricane, the eye, the whole thing. The roof went off where we were, but it was a three-story thing; we had the bottom of the condo that was concrete reinforced, so we felt safe.
>
> But right at dark, right at sunset, it blew over. And so here was this full moon over Makana, because we were up in Princeville. It was over Bali Hai, this full moon, and it looked like a fire had burned the island down. It was splinters.

Cissie also described the immediate aftermath of the storm and the beginning of Kaua'i's restoration:

> It took us three days to get to our home in Ha'ena. There was no road. The locals cleared the road. They got their chainsaws out and all the way from Hanalei, they had to clear. At Lumaha'i, I'll never forget, there was no road. It looked like a path to any park or any wilderness pike. Because the other thing I really remember is there were no leaves on the trees. Everything really looked like a fire. The trees were just sticks. We live in somewhat of a little Hawaiian shack out here, and because it was such an open house, everything just kind of blew through. Everything was ruined, it was wet, it was a mess, but we had a home to come back to. We just pretty much were thankful for that and moved back in and we had gas, so we were ahead of the game. We just got our kerosene lamps and we had gas for cooking and hot water. So, we

felt very blessed. We didn't get water out here in Ha'ena. We had a water truck for months, and we didn't get electricity until Thanksgiving Day. And thank goodness for the military; they came in and saved us. Everything was just leveled. Some houses were gone.

Anytime you went anywhere, there were long lines to use the telephone. It literally took all of the telephone poles. It was wrecked so much that every time you went out, you had a flat tire, there were so many nails on the roads. It was a mess for a really, really long time. The Hanalei Colony was one of the first to reopen, and that was fifteen months later.

Again, credit to Mayor JoAnn Yukimura. She evacuated the tourists. She said, "Please, all visitors leave the island. We don't want you driving around taking pictures," because immediately, people all they wanted to do was drive around and look at the damage and look at the people, and she said no more of that. "All tourists, please leave the island. We need the hotels and the hotel rooms for the people who live here, for the residents to have someplace to stay."

They brought in experts up into Princeville in the big center up there. They brought in all these professionals to help the residents cope with the stress and provide resources and information. One of the things that one of the counselors said was "that everything is going to be hard on your eyes, so try and do something—go somewhere where you're not going to have to look at something that's just demolished." So because I wasn't working, I would go snorkeling. I would go out into the water and I was amazed that there was no debris in the water. The water was clear. Everything else—I don't know where it blew to, blew away, blew inland. The trees were gone and all of that. But the water was clear. The beach had a lot of debris on it, but not underwater.

Bob Eckert was one of the first owners to visit HCR after Iniki:

> As soon as it hit, I tried to book, and it turned out to be the second plane that landed. I remember getting here; what an ordeal! It took hours and hours and hours because although the military had come over and started cleaning up some of the roads—and there was a funny thing, too, it was understood that if somebody's house had been destroyed, if they could push it to the side of the road, the military would clean it up, too, free. Everything was depressing, I had never in my life—and I grew up in Florida and lived through many hurricanes—I had never seen destruction that was everywhere. Of buildings and nature. But the military arrived shortly, and that was one of the positives. There were banners that went up thanking them, and they were young and smiling and they cooked breakfast for us, and they gave us MREs, meals ready to eat, so we could survive doing what we had to do. And just their enthusiasm and the fact that they told us we've been to war zones and we've never seen anything this bad. And yet, it's natural and we're helping people who haven't been shot up. So they gave us morale. They gave us morale.

Dennie and Tom Stansell confirm this:

> It was amazing to see the devastation on the island. The huge piles. I think it was beyond Kapa'a that they had the piles of refrigerators, that kind of thing. There were just mountains of debris. And coming out of Kapa'a, there was some big things on the side of the road.

Dick Moody, who knew what he was talking about from his long experience in the construction business, also visited HCR shortly after the storm. The roads were covered with debris, "the telephone poles, all the big telephone lines were down, but there was enough room to travel, and I did drive from the airport to the units. Had to crisscross around telephone poles, and all the other stuff, but it was worth it to get to the Colony. It was a very sobering site initially."

In an anniversary story a year after the storm, the *San Francisco Chronicle* reported that 150 mph winds had demolished 90 percent of the telephone poles and 1,427 homes, with more than five thousand others sustaining major damage. Seven deaths and $1.8 billion in damage were reported. By all accounts, the people of Kaua'i handled it well. The *Garden Island* reported the experience of a claims coordinator for State Farm Insurance, who had come to Kaua'i directly from Andrew-stricken Florida, and reported, "There's no comparison to the friendliness he has experienced on Kaua'i. The Homestead area in Florida suffered the same kind of devastation, but he thinks the strong family structure and sense of community set Kaua'ians apart in the way they handled the tragedy." In a twenty-year retrospective, *Hawai'i News Now* said, "It was the spirit of Kaua'i's people that fueled the recovery." And in a *Garden Island* article a year after Iniki, Mayor JoAnn Yukimura remembered, "The spirit of Kaua'i was clear and upbeat, even in the midst of the devastation. It was this spirit, the spirit of courage, aloha, and *'ohana*, that would carry us through the days to come."

HCR – The Impact. HCR was severely damaged. Buildings were torn open; building materials and their contents were strewn chaotically across the grounds or beyond. Most roofs were damaged, and interiors were exposed to water. End and side walls on some units were gone. There was no water, no electricity. Power was not restored to HCR until October 22, but even then there were rolling blackouts and low water pressure from time to time. The resort could not accommodate owners or guests, but it didn't matter because no visitors and very few owners were traveling to the island anyway.

Here is how Howard and Averil Koch of unit E-4 describe the damage to the buildings:

> The hurricane came through and ripped all the lanai roofs off the I and J buildings and they crashed into Laura's place,

L-2, and severed the boards that hold the whole thing up. So L-2 was pretty well destroyed. Our building, E, didn't have much damage except a hole in the roof, but this was on the outside, in the eaves, so no water was coming in. One of the picnic tables from the barbecue area went through the end of D building, and you could see the shape of the picnic table in the side of the building. Things were moving at about 175 miles per hour, so it was pretty bad.

Damage to lanais of J and K buildings caused by Iniki, 1992.
(Courtesy Rich Sells)

Dennie and Tom Stansell talked about the damage to their unit, H-2. Dennie recalls: "Somebody told us—and I don't know whether this is true or not—that ours was the only unit that lost the sliding glass doors. The sliding glass doors were blown out, and the hurricane just rolled inside and just took everything. It just looked like a bomb had gone off." A small kindness made a big difference that echoes down to today: "Our guest books, the McGregor sisters found them out in various places around the yard and carefully put tissue paper in between the pages, because they were all soaked. And then dried them out and got them to us when we came over here. That was remarkable. So we still have those at home. A little blurry on some of them."

Dick Moody had mixed emotions: "Iniki left nothing. When that hit, it took my unit, I-4, and blew the porch completely off. I had just built a brand new screen door, some months before. I put the first screen door on that unit, and that blew away; couldn't find that at all. I stayed in the unit next door to I-4 and worked on my own unit to get it livable. But that was a fun time," he laughs. "It was a real mess with tons and tons of huge big trucks coming by, and we'd just throw the roofs on them."

Damage to roof and walls caused by Iniki, 1992. (Courtesy Rich Sells)

Rebuilding did not begin at once, but cleanup did. "Laura Beemer (later, Laura Richards) and Jane Yadao put everything together again. Got things going again real quickly. I was surprised," remembers Dick Moody. The neighbors who lived on the dirt road began calling HCR

"Jane and Laura's Place." Roger Parlee described his first impressions in the board minutes: "Cleanup was started immediately. Efforts were made to try and save the subflooring by removing wet carpet immediately. Tarps were not immediately available. They were finally obtained through Howard Koch."

Howard describes this: "I sent over all of these blue tarps that I could get from Home Depot, and one of our dear friends who was in the shipping business got it over here quickly, and Laura and Jane and the crew put them up on the roofs." Pat Montague recalled, "It was really devastating to see the way they had pulled all the furniture out and the mattresses and everything." By late September, roofers had begun putting up the tarps to cover the buildings. A small staff "stripped the beds and saved the linen. They also cleaned out all the refrigerators and buried the garbage." Routine maintenance, such as grounds and cavitettes (underground sewage treatment devices), also continued. By late November, eight units in buildings C, D, and E were livable, with electricity and plumbing.

Laura Richards remembers that living at HCR immediately following the storm "was quite an experience." She explains:

> First of all, it was an experience because we went from this resort to a broken bones cemetery. We just happened to be tree-trimming right before this happened. So we got to be one of the first properties to do some of the actual cleanup since these machines were here. The next thing we knew, we had debris literally in the courtyard, centering the courtyard, higher than the buildings. So that in itself was amazing. And then, little by little, people started to show up with tarps. The first thing, again, David Swenson and the maintenance staff then were climbing up on the roofs and putting the tarps over. So we spent months and months and months just looking at these dilapidated buildings with tarps over them. We finally got the debris starting to be removed from the center courtyard.
>
> Then we reached the place where we knew we were going to have the new furniture package. So we needed

to get rid of all the old furniture. What an amazing day that was. I had to hire neighborhood people to help me, and we put all the furniture in the five units for the entire resort. It's just stacked. Then I went down to the Wainiha store and I told Janet that on this day, at this time, that we were going to have a furniture giveaway. It's whatever you want. It was going to start at ten in the morning on a Saturday. At 6:00 a.m., the parking lot was full. Everybody had the biggest truck that they could possibly find. They had ropes. They had wagons. It was hysterical. So we ended up opening the doors at about 8:45 a.m. By ten in the morning, there was nothing left. Everybody left here looking like the Beverly Hillbillies. It was an amazing thing to see.

A few people lived at the resort immediately following the storm. Permanent HCR residents Mary and Dee McGregor, in units A-2 and E-3, and Dale Koeppe, in unit M-2, returned to the resort shortly after the hurricane passed. Mary then left the resort until the rebuild was complete, but Dale and Dee remained at the resort throughout the rebuild. Mary remembers that although it took quite a while to fix Dee's apartment, her telephone continued to work. So everyone went to her place to use the telephone. Mary and Dee both came out of the devastation with shiny souvenirs. The company that was refurbishing hotels had "two mirrors left that the hotels didn't want," so Dee got them. Mary is still delighted with the one on her wall. Peter Kelly, a local man who had lost his home in the storm and was working at HCR, also stayed at the resort with his son. At the time of the storm, Laura Beemer (later, Laura Richards) was resident manager, living in unit L-2. But L-2 was destroyed in the hurricane, so she and her husband, Peter, and her two boys lived in unit C-1 for thirteen months. They were soon to be joined by many others, but not by your usual sort of owners and guests!

All of the island hotels and resorts sustained some level of damage. Most closed altogether for a period of time, but a few stayed partially open while reconstruction went on. Laura Richards recalls that the Hyatt had half of the resort open; they charged ninety-eight dollars for every room. "It was so funny, because there were no guests coming to the island. But all of us were like, 'Oh my God, we'll do anything to see some sort of normal in our life.' We'd go to the Hyatt, so all your friends were at the Hyatt." The old Hilton, now the Aqua Beach Resort, was, she says, "Pretty much dripping all the way, but they were open. However, they weren't open to the public; all the insurance people stayed there." Some hotels gradually opened as repairs were completed "in little pods. It's like OK, well, we have these buildings ready. In many cases when they opened they didn't open on time. So everywhere you went, it was still construction all over," Laura recalls. But HCR was the first resort to open with all its facilities repaired and ready to receive guests. It opened on schedule, November 20, 1993.

In late September, not long after the storm, the board members visited HCR for a day to view the damage and prepare reports for the owners. They flew in on a special flight from Honolulu to Princeville. The next day, the joint boards of the AOAO and the rental program met formally in Honolulu in the offices of our local advertising agent, DiCarlo & Woodrum. The rental program was suspended, and owner visits were limited to daytime. A period of intense organization, planning, and decision making began. Bill Hayward chaired a restoration committee with owners Dick Rainforth and Jim Perzick.

HCR – The Recovery. The management of the rebuild—the fact that it happened at all—was a marvel. It required that our insurance provider, our project management firm, and the construction company come together quickly and efficiently. The insurance coverage itself involved a stroke of good fortune, as well as good management. Without it, there might not have been enough money to pay for rebuilding. There was a very real possibility that the insurance company would refuse to cover the full loss. As Tom Stansell put it:

> The board had decided to go with a different insurance company the month before the hurricane hit. The new company immediately looked around the property and

gave us a quick estimate of what it would be and said, "Sign here." The board, very fortunately, and thanks very largely to Bill Hayward, who was vice president at this time, said, "No, thank you, we'll do a little more investigating." Again thanks to Bill Hayward, they hired a company out of Honolulu.

This was Rider Hunt Construction Services, now Rider Levett Bucknall, a global construction and management company that traces its roots back to an English surveying firm in 1785 and has been involved in some of the most significant engineering projects of the last three centuries. We were in very good hands. Rider Hunt provided us with professional project management services and represented us with the insurance adjuster. Our new insurance broker was Jerry Hay, Inc., of Honolulu. Janne Hayward recalls that, prophetically, we had switched to the new broker because it provided us with business interruption insurance, which had not been available through our previous broker. This product was now very much appreciated. Our new insurance company, First Hawaiian Insurance, was represented by Rick Kuzmanoff. We also relied on a public adjuster, the Alex Sill Company, for support in interpreting our insurance policies.

Tom Stansell describes the next steps toward reconstruction:

> Bill Hayward and the rest of the board hired Rider Hunt to come over. They surveyed the property, and made a book on every single unit of what went wrong: a huge, huge thing. They went with us to this brand new insurance company and said, "Your offer—thank you very much, but it's not enough. Here's our documentation; we need this much money to rebuild this place." The insurance company said, "There's no way in the world we could possibly dispute this, so here's a check." They gave us the money.

What happened was that Tony Smith from Rider Hunt went through every unit and made detailed lists of all the specific damage and what it would cost to replace it. The list was "two hundred pages of line-by-line detail of the work to be done," according to the minutes of a November meeting of the combined boards. He then went through this record with the agent from the First Insurance Company of Hawai'i. It was this review that convinced the insurance company to settle. Howard Koch, who was president at the time, also recalls that story:

> This guy from the insurance company came out, and our insurance agent over in Oahu, Chris York [with Jerry Hay, Inc.], who had visited HCR immediately following the storm and knew about the severity of the damage, was trying to show him what the problems were here, and he told Chris York to pack it up or something. Rider Hunt had a figure somewhere about $2,250,000, and the insurance company thought it was $550,000. When this agent from the insurance company started talking about the $550,000, this fella from Rider Hunt said to him, "Come with me," and took him to every building and showed him the damage, and pretty soon this guy started thinking, *Uh, maybe I've got to come up with some more money.* Actually, I give credit to Bill Hayward and Jim Perzik for getting this representative from the insurance company to finally say, "Whatever it takes, we'll do."

In the end, the insurance company agreed to pay $1.8 million. Finally we had the necessary funding to rebuild HCR. It is hard to imagine what the future of HCR would have been without the insurance settlement to pay for the rebuild. Tom Stansell recalls, "Bill Hayward was very much responsible for this. He had Rider Hunt find the construction company that would rebuild this place. They found a construction company in Utah." This was the Bud Bailey Construction Company of Salt Lake City. The architect was Neil Hudson from Honolulu (ironically located on Wainiha Street). The rapid rebuild was largely attributable to the insurance settlement, Rider Hunt's management, and Bud Bailey's execution. We are indebted to these firms, and we continue to work with what is now the firm of Rider Levett Bucknall. Chris York, says:

> The heroes of the Iniki rebuild were the board of directors and the owners who helped them—Bunny Alexander, Robert Ebert, Bob Eckert, Scott Fladgard, Bill Hayward, Janne Hayward, Howard Koch, Pat Montague, Roger Parlee, Jim Perzik, Dick Rainforth. They were proactive and effectively managed the insurance companies.

Janne Hayward points out that the board "did not so much manage the insurance companies as it did the flow of information to the owners, the care of employees, and the future of the property."

In December 1992, after the settlement of the insurance matter and the selection of the management and construction companies, Howard Koch resigned from the board, and Dick Rainforth (known fondly at HCR as "the Colonel" for his service in the US Marine Corps) stepped in as president. When Jane Yadao resigned, Laura Beemer (later, Laura Richards) was put in charge of rebuilding the resort, and in 1993, Dick Rainforth appointed Laura general manager. Scott Fladgard was appointed construction liaison with Rider Hunt. Construction was estimated to start in mid-March and to last five to seven months. Work began on March 30. As Tom Stansell recalls:

> The construction company in Utah came over with lots of workers and settled into whichever units were livable enough to be here. They started reconstructing the place. Laura didn't have any guests, of course, other than these people. So on weekends she would have big bonfires out on the beach and things like that to keep people feeling like this was a friendly, nice place. We got this place back better than it had been before the hurricane.

It *was* better. Not only was it rebuilt, but the ongoing reconstruction provided an opportunity to offer owners options and upgrades at very favorable rates. These included windows and kitchen conversions.

Laura describes the beginning of reconstruction:

> We sat for months with nothing going on, and then all of a sudden, one day out of nowhere, this trailer arrived and parked in front of the E building. That was the trailer for the company that we had hired to come in and start the construction. About a week after that, thirteen or fourteen young whippersnapper men showed up, and they started redoing the roofs. That was a pretty amazing thing because, again, they didn't have big equipment yet that they could bring in here. So these guys were literally carrying and climbing a ladder up to the roof edge, where there was no roof, carrying beams big enough that they could throw a beam to go all the way down across one-half the side of the roof. I don't even know how it went, but we watched that. The construction company was wonderful. Well, between the construction company and also Rider Hunt. Tony Smith is who we worked with through Rider Hunt. He was here all the time, and he made things move. He was great. He lived in Honolulu, so he'd fly in once a week. Because what would happen is you have all these change orders going on all the time. Like here's the plan, and then every time we got into a unit, then the contractors would come to me and say, "Well, we need to do this, but we don't need to do that." We would set the change orders, and then Tony would come in and renegotiate how it would affect anything or not. And we all worked really well together.

The roof of A building undergoing repair following Iniki damage. Note heavily denuded ironwood trees. (Courtesy HCR Archives)

But it wasn't all work all the time, according to Laura:

> They built in the center of the courtyard a huge skateboard ramp. Think about it. Now, suddenly we have fourteen, fifteen, then we had twenty, twenty-five… shortly, we had up to about forty men living here, and they all lived in the D building and the E building. They were bored to tears, so they would work hard all day and then they'd drink hard all afternoon and they'd skateboard and would do flips—I mean, they were really talented skateboarders. I had to go out and get my kids head-to-toe skateboard equipment because they thought this is the greatest thing in the world. So they were out there learning how to do flips on this ramp. So that was their entertainment. [To this day, Laura's son Peter (PC) Beemer gleefully recalls learning to skateboard on the

half-pipe with the construction workers.] On Fridays, every Friday, they got to have a big steak dinner. The resort would host it or I would take them over there and host a big dinner for them at the pool, buy them beer and everything they wanted. They'd tear that place apart and they'd get so crazy, but it didn't matter because they had to put it back together.

Bob Eckert confirms this optimistic approach to the job:

I would say we had trouble even inspiring each other. Except Laura, who was such a heroine. It seems to me that she managed to smile and see the best side of things. Laura said to the board, "Well, you call this a hard job? I wake up, and I go out there, and there are about twelve good-looking, young, eager repairmen from Utah smiling all day long, and I'm the only woman around? That's not a job; that's a picnic.

Construction workers' laundry drying on walkway of D building. (Courtesy HCR Archives)

Then there was a special treat at the end of the job, described by Laura:

> Then, before we reopened, we went down and we had a five-day camp-out at the end of the road, because at that time, we could still drive down toward Taylor Camp. I went down there, and I set up a full camp with kayaks and all kinds of rental equipment. I set up a full kitchen, bought all the food, and I cooked breakfast, lunch, and dinner for different people who came in and out. They would stay for about two or three days. We were there for five or six days. And all these construction workers would come down and rent it. It was kind of our gift to them to have a couple of days off and come down and play. I took care of them, and that was, that was really fun, too. Living here with about sixteen men was quite an adventure.

Looking back from twenty years later, Laura muses:

> I don't want to do it again; I'm glad I didn't miss it. I mean, it was phenomenal. We were so blessed. But we were here living in warm weather, and who cares if you don't have hot water, and who cares if you don't have electricity? I called it living on the halftime, because you can only get done half of what you thought you were going to get done. That was a big time here for the resort. Clearly. I mean, it could easily have gone awry in a number of different ways.

Camp-out at Ke'e Beach for construction workers to celebrate completion of reconstruction of Iniki damage. (Courtesy HCR Archives)

The reopening celebration in 1993 was especially memorable. It coincided with the Thanksgiving Day holiday. About half of the owners were present. Chris York, Tony Smith, and others from the rebuilding team also attended, as did the mayor, JoAnn Yukimura. Tom Stansell remembers:

> There was a ceremony that Laura had arranged for us to go into the courtyard, and we were all standing around holding hands. Both a Hawaiian and a Christian woman came out and did blessings for the land. We took a branch off to the corners of the property and planted it. It was a new growth or renewal symbol. I went with one of the other people on the board, and we did that to symbolize that this place was going to come back to life again.

And there was a big dinner in the evening. "We all pitched in and cooked. And that was fun," recalls Nancee Sells. It was a very emotional experience, as Bob Eckert meditates:

> But just reopening, being together, starting up when so many other things were still closed, it was—what do you call it? It was like a resurrection; it was just a very, very powerful, overwhelmingly emotional, and beautiful

experience. This was more than fun, this went to my soul, every fiber of my being; it was just powerful.

When HCR came back to life, it came back richer, more vibrant, and more alive.

Chapter 11
Talk Story—The People

A couple who have been a part of HCR for many years are on their lanai having a quiet supper with a few friends to celebrate their anniversary. Their next-door neighbor happens by, carrying his Hanalei Dolphin grocery bag. They call him over. He opens his bag and offers everyone a selection from the sushi he bought. Their upstairs neighbors return from the Wishie Washie Hale with their bag of clean clothes. They run upstairs to fetch some mochi and a platter of mango slices to offer around. Their neighbors from across the grassy courtyard see the growing group and wave. An answering wave calls them over. They bring along a bag of taro chips from Hanalei Poi Company and a pitcher of pineapple juice from the Farmer's Market. The night manager passes on her evening grounds walk. She stops to chat. Through only a few degrees of separation, this group knows many, many people from HCR's extended family. And they remember many, many stories.

Inevitably someone says, "Hey, do you remember the guy who fell in the stream?" or, "Do you remember all those Thanksgiving dinners?" or, "When did your kids first come here without you?" When HCR folk talk story, the number of stories and memories involving other people is a dramatic demonstration of how much its people contribute to making HCR what it is. They talk about friends and family, about guests and the community. They revel in anecdotes about the characters and heroes that have peopled HCR's history. (By the way, a board member—who shall remain nameless—actually did fall into the stream.)

The people of HCR are long-term owners, newbies, guests, neighbors, absentees, full-time residents, frequent visitors, staff, and newly arrived guests. These are all part of HCR's extended family, its *'ohana*. The history of HCR is inseparable from the people who gave it birth and those who live and work and visit here today. These people include the builders with a vision of what could be created at Kepuhi Point and the knowledge and skills needed to bring it into being. They include the early HCR owners and their staff who organized HCR and looked after it and who created the rental program and built a business to support and enhance the resort. They include the people who continue to nurture and preserve HCR. They include all the people who have come to experience the spirit of HCR and to express that spirit. They are the HCR community.

Guests

Guests have always been an important part of the HCR community, and sometimes they have made permanent contributions. "There was a lot of togetherness with the guests and owners," says Aggie Parlee. She describes how some guests from Canada planted seedlings that grew up to become the foliage along the fence by the highway and how a guest from Alaska, an expert on soil, made recommendations on erosion control that were eventually adopted. Cissie Meyer gives an example of guests being part of the HCR family: "Some of our returning guests—we get a lot of them—are special people as well. There's a couple of them that have decided that they can come and spend a month or two months now instead of being owners. But they have that same extended *'ohana* concern about the property and the staff."

Bob Johnstone relates a typical story:

> I had a good interaction with a guest a couple of weeks ago. I met a lady on the beach, and she said her husband was out fishing. We talked to her for a while. That evening, we got a knock at the door, and the guy brought me enough mahimahi (dolphinfish) and tuna to probably last eight dinners.

Carl Woodbury tells of a couple that visits his suite every year. They come in January and stay for three months. "I understand he goes around planting plants. He owns a nursery. He actually brings dishes; they bring silk plants. They bring all sorts of stuff that they keep here. And then, they turn it into their house." It is interesting to see that some guests have returned two, three, five, even twenty times. Cissie Meyer finds that just being in the office and seeing guests there is fun. "On a weekly basis, there's some fun story to share with someone."

The beauty of HCR combined with the seclusion provided by its remote location might well be expected to appeal to celebrities looking to get away from the obligations of celebrity. Indeed, HCR attracts many artists and performers. Sometimes these guests will make the reservation using an alias, and the staff will silently recognize them when they check in—or they might let the staff know that they want to be anonymous. Their confidentiality is respected. In other cases, there is no attempt at anonymity, and the guests actively participate in resort activities. Numerous stories are told. It is said that a professional basketball player meditated on his big career choice while sitting on the lanai of an HCR unit, perhaps J-1. One international film actor rented unit G-2 simply to use as a beach cabana for the day while he stayed elsewhere. Some of these stories have gained the status of legend, if not myth. We have previously heard about partying with Robert Mitchum, but some interactions with Mr. Mitchum were more relaxed, as Claire Walker remembers: "He and Dorothy liked to stay here, and they wanted to go on the helicopter tour," Clair recalls. "He said, 'Will you make the reservations for us in your name and go with us?' So we did. And that was most enjoyable. He was just so pleasant, and she's a sweetheart. But it was kind of fun because he was just in his tennies and his baseball cap. On the way home, we stopped at Foodland and he's just strolling along; nobody recognized him at all."

Bob Eckert also had a touching personal moment with Mr. Mitchum. Eckert's mother had long been a fan of Robert Mitchum because she felt he looked like Bob's dad. The day after the "Mitchum Pool Party," there was a small, private party with more intimate conversation. Mrs. Mitchum invited Bob Eckert to visit them at their ranch. This led Bob to feel a bit closer to Mr. and Mrs. Mitchum, but he did not feel comfortable asking for an autograph. However, "One will do all kinds of difficult things for one's mom," Bob says. So when he happened to be in the office while they were checking out, Bob approached Mr. Mitchum and asked, "Robert, may I ask you for your autograph—for my mom because she really likes you and thinks my father looks like you and she would love to have your autograph?"

"Oh, of course," Mitchum responded. He reached into his briefcase, pulled out a photograph of himself, and said, "What is your mother's first name?"

"Gladys," Eckert answered. So Mitchum wrote on the photo, "Dear Gladys, get a hold of yourself. Love, Robert." That photo remained on the wall of his parents' motel office for the next twenty years until the property was sold.

Then there are the stories about Elizabeth Taylor and Richard Burton at HCR. Indeed, their visit was recorded in the *Garden Island*. Bob Eckert heard the story from the previous owner of his apartment (G-3), Patrick Olds, who told him:

> Liz and Richard stayed in G-3, but they booked the whole building. She brought her children, who stayed downstairs, and his children stayed down in the other unit downstairs. Next to me, in G-4, her press secretary stayed. She spent a month. A housekeeper who was there at the time later told me that the staff was thinking, *Oh my goodness, we are going to have a lot of work because she's been in there a month.* But they walked in and it was spotless. All the dishes were done—I'm guilty of not having time or a desire to do that myself, but Liz Taylor cleans house and washes dishes. They said, "On the other hand, she's a bit flighty because she would go on the lanai in the morning when the sun was coming up over Princeville and she'd take photos using her flash. And the flash would shine across the stream over to the J and the K building and she would do that repeatedly." Then after a while, they said, "Oh, guess what? It's not a flashcube; it's that ring. The sun is hitting it and sending a flash across the stream."

An article in the *Garden Island* confirmed the story of the visit. Liz did the cooking, and they left the place in "glorious order." The article did not mention the ring.

Richard Burton once ran into Dave Ballard, Mary McGregor's husband, on the beach. Dave was a radio announcer, famous for his reading voice, and Richard Burton, of course, was also famous for his voice. Once they recognized each other, it is said, they both burst into enthusiastic expressions of how much they admired each other's work.

Guests and owners are an important part of the staff's experience; guests are much more than just customers. Says Tommy Richards:

> It is pretty nice because a lot of guests come every year or every other year. I got to know quite a few of them, and it is really nice being able to share the aloha spirit with them because, obviously, where they live, it may not be so prevalent. But between the owners and the employees, it is just a great big family.

Friends and Neighbors

Owners often express a distinct sense of friendship within the HCR community. For example, Chuck Williams says,

> Fifteen years or more, we've always been coming over in November, and so, during that same time frame, a lot of other owners who happen to pick that time of year are always here. So we have gotten to know very well people like Howard and Averil Koch and Jack and Vivian Caldwell. So it makes it fun because it's like coming back each year and having a little reunion with people we don't know the rest of the year. It's like coming home to family and seeing these other people that we really enjoy.

Cissie Meyer gives another example. "Howard and Averil are very, very special to me and dear to my heart. I really feel that they are the true meaning of extended *'ohana*." For Linda Stoskopf, "Meeting our friends in a different environment and enjoying afternoon cocktails or dinner is just fun. I feel so fortunate to be able to have that kind of experience." Darrel Stoskopf feels that through owners' meetings, "we have gotten to know all the owners for the most part; it is really like a family and I look forward to going there just to see friends." Pat Montague feels that it was "really great for me to be on the board after Morgan died, because I came over here for the meetings. It was like having a whole neighborhood of friends to go to. Coming over here and making friends will always be special to me." Dennie Stansell recalls that "having girlfriends here, that was good. Just to get together. We had a great time with them here. That's a very fond memory." Tom agrees with his wife, saying,

> Your girlfriends coming over are some of your fondest memories. Because you all would sit around on the lanai and drink coffee and things like that. So, she has a group of three women—the four of them are the Ya-Yas—and they've come over now two or maybe three times.

Aggie Parlee expresses this simply and powerfully. "There was a time when I felt like we had more friends here in Kaua'i than in Honolulu [their home]."

Unexpected connections among the people of HCR, sometimes uncanny connections, have occurred over the years. Janne Hayward describes one of her fondest memories:

> You sit around the barbecue and you talk story with people. The seven degrees of separation, it's just always been fascinating to me when somebody is there for meetings and you get talking and suddenly you know somebody that they know. It's this small-world aspect of things.

Cissie Meyer confirms this small-world phenomenon. She tells about a local woman who once worked in the HCR office and had a family connection to Brazil. The woman had made reservations for her brother, a professional athlete. As Cissie was checking him in, she mentioned that back in the 1970s she was living at Sunset Beach on Oahu and one of the fellows who shared the house was also from Brazil. It turned out that the fellow from Sunset Beach was now a famous TV producer who was the best friend of the guest! So now Cissie has a standing invitation to Rio. John Brekke has a similar story:

> So actually, I started to get to know people around here, "Hi, what's up, how's it going today?" We sit and chat for a little while. So I go to music festivals, and there's one in California called Coachella. I was wearing my Waipa tank top. And I was standing there listening to this great music, having a great time dancing, and all of a sudden this guy walks up behind me and he goes, "Hey, dude, do you like walking along the beach in Hanalei?" This was Palm Springs. And I go, "Oh yeah, I go over there as much as I can and I do that every night at sunset." He goes, "I know you." I said, "Really?" So, he was the guy that lives on the beach around here. In his twenties, makes a trip over to Coachella every year, I guess. Damnedest thing.

How about this coincidence? I once needed a book to read, so I checked out a mystery novel from the HCR library in the office. As soon as I got back to California, the film version of the novel appeared on TV. It starred Pierce Brosnan, whom I, of course, had met at the Mediterranean Gourmet. (Sadly, the plot had nothing to do with Kaua'i.)

The HCR small-world experience includes guests. Consider this entry left in an owner's guest book: "Our biggest surprise was discovering that our best friends from New Hampshire [their home] had been in this very same condo last June. Talk about a small world!"

HCR is pretty well integrated into the local neighborhood. So a lot of interaction occurs among the HCR folk and our neighbors. Owners not only have memories of such occasions but continue to interact with the folks nearby. Several HCR staff live in the neighborhood, and local residents have long worked at HCR. Alicia Cortrite remembers her friend, a local woman named Rekha Sharma, who performed weddings and was the person at the pool who did lei making and organized breakfast parties for HCR. At one time, as Alicia says, Rekha also operated a Keiki Club, or children's club, for the guests. Alicia explains:

> You just signed up in the front office, and you could leave your kids. She had a room; it wasn't necessarily the same room, but one of the units that happened to be available. They would watch movies. They would do art projects; they would make leis and make shell necklaces. She was a big part of our lives here.

Rekha also taught Georgia Henry's granddaughter the hula.

Mary McGregor recalls frequent *pau hana* (quitting time) hukilaus, where our neighbors from up and down the beach would come to her apartment and catch fish right in front of the resort: "End of the week, and they would bring their nets right out here and someone would be up a tree watching, watching, watching, and then finally they'd say, 'Get out there; the fish are there.' They'd pull in the net and there'd be a ton of fish."

The ladies would go into the water in their mu'umu'us (loose gowns). People brought hibachis to cook the fresh fish. People would come from all around when they smelled the fish cooking. People would sit around and play music and sing. They had beautiful voices. They had a washboard band with ukuleles and a washtub broomstick string base—a gut bucket—and kids would bang along on stuff, making their own music on the way to growing up into skilled musicians themselves. Guests at the resort would run to listen in to the music. Everybody would come here for the entertainment—and the food. Leftover fish were distributed, and Mary could eat for days.

Hukilau at Kepuhi Beach, winter 1970–1971. (Courtesy Mary McGregor)

As manager of HCR, Georgia Henry often relied on our neighbors, and they relied on HCR. Georgia gives an example:

> We were the last resort here. Our neighbors were very close to us, and every time there was a flood down the road where there is a very low area, I would have them come and stay the night until they could get back into their houses. We hired several of them from time to time for various things. One of them we hired to clear out the mouth of the creek that was completely dammed up. We had other neighbors performing different jobs for us—plumbing for one.

She feels that the local people were "watching over us so that nothing ever happened."

Nancee Sells tells about hanging out with some local residents they met casually:

> We met some local folks out on the beach who were fishing for sea urchins using wire cages. We were out there with our children. They invited us to their house for dinner. They lived up Powerhouse Road. They served turkey butts and sea urchins. They took us around the

property—one of those where the creek runs through. He was doing some fishing and raising shrimp.

Nancee once went to a local lu'au "just on the other side of the first little bridge with Georgia Henry when she was manager. My daughter was with me. That was an interesting evening, too. Because we had never done anything like that."

"It's always been kind of really friendly, and I've gotten to know a lot of people in the neighborhood and those that work here. So I really like it," says Carl Woodbury. He gives a few examples:

> Well, I found out that there is a huge San Francisco 49ers fan contingent here. So I'll be going to Hanalei to watch the games if we can't see them here. Right now I am also borrowing a bike from one of the local residents so I can get around. The local neighbors are just very friendly when I see them out and about. Stop and talk all the time, you know? I get a lot of good advice about places I might go see: places up on the mountain to hike and waterfalls to go see and places to kayak and stuff that maybe you wouldn't normally see in a guidebook somewhere. So it's been cool. And certainly, a lot of people live just down the block from here that work here, right next door, as a matter of fact.

Welcoming and hospitality toward guests are a deep part of Hawaiian culture and are often expressed by the local community. Mary McGregor's son Mike Ballard, with his wife and another couple, arrived for a two-week vacation courtesy of Mary and Dave. They were greeted by Auntie Louise, Barlow Chew, and two other local people. "Flowers, music, and much food were also part of the greeting," Mike remembers fondly. They only saw their welcome committee that night, "but every morning for the rest of the two-week stay, fresh fruit was on the deck."

Family

Many HCR owners, of course, are members of their own extended and blended families. The families often include two or more generations. This long-term commitment reflects the deep-rooted importance of HCR to these families. HCR responds to this commitment by providing for the needs of each generation. As we see throughout this history, many owners and guests have affectionate memories of family events and often express their sense that the HCR environment contributes to family solidity.

Dennie and Tom Stansell relate how "Laura Richards was born and raised in Lynchburg, Virginia, which is in the mountains, not far from where I grew up, and Tommy Richards, of course, was a military kid in Yorktown, I think. Which is where my sister lives now. So not only did I find home, I found home folks." Home folks are almost like family. And this feeling of family permeates the experience of the folks who make up the HCR family—its *'ohana nui*.

Weddings are often the paramount ceremony in family history. HCR is a place for romance, so weddings at HCR may be a natural phenomenon. Carol and Jim Thompson are probably one of the first couples who were married at HCR. They had won a week on Kaua'i in a silent auction at a charity event. "Not just anywhere in the Islands, but a week on Kaua'i for $100," says Carol, grinning. Unfortunately, the prize was at Po'ipu, and they were not happy with the crowding and the traffic. They had been visiting HCR for a number of years, so they called to see if they could come up there after Po'ipu. They could, and it would be the beginning of big things.

While still at Po'ipu, they said to each other, "While we're here, why don't we get married?" They had actually planned ahead and had gotten their blood tests and paperwork in order but had made no arrangements for the ceremony. So in the moment, they faced the question, "On Kaua'i, who do you call for a marriage license?" In the phone book they found a lady who gave them directions to her house, where they worked out the details at a picnic table in her backyard. "That is the bureaucracy here in Kaua'i for getting married. We thought that was charming," recalls Jim.

Fern Michaels, a local minister and wedding organizer, came up to HCR to conduct the wedding. "We recruited Bob and Nella Ebert to stand up with us. We had gotten to know each other just passing around the resort. We went down on the beach in front of Bob and Nella's unit [I-1]." There was first a traditional wedding and then a Hawaiian ceremony. Carol remembers, "This is where they ask the earth, and the sky, and the wind, and the ocean if it's OK for us to become a couple. Fern took in the response and said, 'Yes, they agree this will work.'" Jim continues, "Then she started some chants, and it was very delightful. We went barefoot to our own wedding and are still living happily ever after."

Janne Hayward's fondest memory is of

> the people who would come year after year and then finally bought a place. That's always fun. To watch the kids grow; to watch people on the board who had young kids, and watch them get older, and see them come back for their honeymoons, or bring their kids. That's always fun.

Indeed, in 2013, three of the seven members of the board of directors were children of prior owners.

A large part of the family experience at HCR is sharing it with children. Almost everyone has commented nostalgically on watching and playing with their children in the HCR environment. Alicia Cortrite says she has loved "watching my children grow up over here. And year to year appreciating it in such different ways is the most fun thing. It's an ongoing process of fun." Moreen William describes her fondest memory: "Having our kids here with us when they were still in junior high and high school. And coming here as a family and just really relaxing and doing things as a family, just locally here." Georgia Henry says, "Oh, I was able to have my granddaughter with me on her eighteenth birthday. And also my daughter came with her two-year-old, and I had her with me, too. Those are certainly memorable to me." People bring their kids to HCR because it is a safe and stimulating environment for them. Nancy Sells says,

> Whenever we would come and bring our children, there were always other kids here that our kids would get acquainted with, and you did not worry about your children. I never worried about them at all. They could be out in that creek bed or running up and down the beach. We just didn't worry about them. And they loved it because Mom wasn't running after them going, "Where are you? What are you doing?"

Molly Ksander introduced her youngest grandson to the ocean at HCR when he was fifteen months old. "It was like *Oh wow!* I mean, this is a scary ocean, it has big waves and riptide. His eyes and the light! We had to literally scoop him up or he was going to go head first into the waves and never be seen again. He's been a water boy ever since." Her seven-year-old granddaughter also took to the north shore waters. She had never snorkeled, so her dad and uncle took her over to HCR's pool with her snorkel gear for a bit of practice. "The next thing you know, they're chasing turtles off of Ke'e."

Marion Burns says, "Well, my fondest memories were the fact that I used to bring my kids here, and they grew up here. And then I would take my grandkids there. So it's been a family history." At the core of all these experiences is simply the opportunity to be with your children, as Tom Stansell dreamily recalls:

> Playing with my children has been fantastic. I had a wonderful trip without Dennie here, but with our two grandchildren from San Diego. I determined that that week was going to be all about play. We just did everything we could, ATVs, swimming, snorkeling, tubing. The biggest fun my granddaughter had was when I took them deep sea fishing. She doesn't smile a lot, but man, she couldn't stop smiling on this fishing trip. Everybody

> was amazed and then began to stand back and let her just catch one fish after another. She'd throw the line in, pull another fish in. Throw the line out, another fish would come in. She just could not stop grinning; it was incredible. It was just a neat, neat time. Everything about that was a smiley time.

Other memories, some of these extremely moving, are of special family events, holidays, and celebrations, especially birthdays and Christmas. Janne Hayward remembers a special birthday:

> Bill's children, as they were in their college years, had not come back very often. The two grandchildren from the Boston area had never been to the resort. The whole family came out for Bill's birthday in 2010. They got up the first morning, the oldest grandkids, and they said, "How come we've never been here before?" So they keep whining and saying, "Let's go back to Hawai'i." It was just so fun to watch people gather in the courtyard and play Frisbee and do whatever. You know, hang out together.

Averil Koch says, "I gave Howard a surprise birthday party here. I brought all of the kids over and I paid for it myself. He didn't know anyone was coming. Anyway, he came in, and he says, 'What are you doing here?' You know?"

Alicia Cortrite is emotionally moved as she remembers "a really special Christmas":

> Al was my stepfather. My father has been over here quite a bit as well. So Dad was here; and Mother and Al; and my husband, Mike, and myself; and Mike's and my kids. We decorated a branch that Mother found on the beach with origami and all sorts of things that she'd brought over. Unlike our huge Christmases at her huge house in Pasadena, it was just so simple and so few presents. The

kids appreciated that so much. It was so fun to see that Christmas the way Christmas should be.

Claire Walker has many fond memories of children, especially at Christmas:

> Well, there's so many fond memories. We came over so many times with our family, our two daughters. One Christmas, I remember, we shipped our station wagon over from Oahu on Young Brothers. I think Catherine was eleven; Kylie was about nine. We loaded it up with Christmas presents and came over to spend Christmas and New Year's, and it rained the whole time. We found a little Norfolk pine Christmas tree in Hanalei town—and we ended up decorating that. But we spent most of the time right in the condo with puzzles and reading and things like that.

This family spirit carries over to the people who work at HCR and may be partially responsible for the presence of multiple generations of the same family working here. Laura Richards describes the informal, family oriented atmosphere long present among the staff:

> But the family feeling was there. For a number of years, it was Cissie, myself, and a woman named Chris Bryan. Chris and I both had young children. So we had the pleasure of knowing the kids could jump on the school bus. And of course, I was living here for many of those years. But even when I didn't live here, they'd jump off the school bus. They'd all play in the courtyard until we got off work, and they'd run in and out like little ragamuffins.

Now those kids are a grown-up part of the HCR family. Members of Laura Richards's family have contributed broadly to the resort. Her step-daughter, Yarrow, and Yarrow's husband, Imad, of course, operate the

Mediterranean Gourmet, and her son, Peter, with a wife and children of his own, works there from time to time. Another son, Leland, also works at the resort.

Laura also tells about Glenda Diego, a local resident who worked for a time in the HCR front office and the laundry area. Her mother, Gonie Diego, had also been a member of the HCR staff. Laura Richards recalls, "Glenda started coming here with her mother [Gonie]. She was probably two or three years old, and she would just come to work with her mom, and then she ended up working in the laundry room for a number of years."

Cissie Meyer tells a similar two-generation story:

> When I started here at the desk, one of the housekeepers that is now working here again, we call her Honey Honey [Poni'moi]. You will know her as Honey. Her mother, Pua [Rose], and her father, Joe [Dorian], were the night resident managers at the time. They actually lived in M-2. She spent the first five years of her life here. We all knew her as Thamie Jo, this little girl with the dark curls. When I was in housekeeping in the 1980s, she was just a little thing, three years old. Joe was a musician; he played at Tahiti Nui with the other Honey Girl and her uncle Peter. All the old-timers that used to go to Tahiti Nui knew him. Joe was part of that musical family. So talk about full circle! I could imagine how Thamie Jo Honey feels being back here. This was one of her first homes.

Cissie sees that the extended *'ohana* feeling illustrates "how you keep a personal staff, and can take pride in your staff. That they're actually bringing to work something more than just punching a clock. They're actually bringing care and love with them to their jobs. And real feeling. I hope it never loses that aspect of the job."

That feeling flows through to the owners. Molly Ksander cannot single out a most notable staff member. "Everybody who works there, every housekeeper, groundskeeper…the list of names is too long. But every time you're there, they welcome you home, and you really feel it. You really care what happens to them and want to do what you can to keep it all in the family. That's the *'ohana* of the place."

Then, too, even the extra-terrestrial Stitch also found his *'ohana* on the north shore in the 2002 film *Lilo & Stitch*.

HCR is a family place and a place for family. Alicia Cortrite expresses this with eloquence and nostalgia: "I cannot imagine a place in the world that has so much heart. I just can't thank my mother enough for falling in love with it. Because I certainly hope it will be in my family and in my brother's family for years and years and years and years to come. It's a special place."

Community

When people have something in common and, especially, when they get together again and again, they become a community. An unexpected consequence of HCR is that it brings together people who would never cross paths in the everyday world. As Molly Ksander asks and answers, "What is the one common thing that has us all sitting in this room together, passionately caring about what we're doing? It's the place." Owners, guests, and staff mix, as do mainlanders and Kaua'ians, easterners and westerners, northern Californians and southern. So the HCR community is particularly diverse. The spell of HCR has captivated all these individuals and had bound them into a single community in which their personal interests and their shared needs merge.

People often comment on the diversity of HCR folk. This diversity is witnessed by the variety of comments expressed throughout this history. Often, this diversity has itself been the occasion for amusement. The contrasts, oddly, can be bonding. Molly Ksander, John Brekke, and Rich Sells—with an occasional assist from Carl Woodbury—have entertained many an owners' dinner with good-natured repartee over—let us say— "politically sensitive" topics. When Rich completed a term as president of the board of directors, he was playfully rewarded with a T-shirt he certainly could not wear around his Southern California friends and neighbors. Politics and philosophy can, indeed, beget humor. This diversity also brings a wide range of talent, skills, and experience that enables HCR to thrive. Molly Ksander describes that diversity:

> It's just the mix of the different owners and the something special that each one of them brings to the mix; preciseness and enthusiasm; deep history of the area; and involvement with the local people. Other people who have been there forever capture the spirit of appreciating where you are and what you're doing at the very moment.

Gatherings and celebrations are both the result of community consciousness and part of the glue that joins the community together. This is very true of HCR. I wrote earlier about memorable pool parties. Everyone has a personal favorite party recollection. Aggie Parlee recalls that "we could really relax" at parties following board meetings. She particularly remembers how much fun theme parties were—a cowboy dress-up party especially stands out. On occasion, the people at HCR would be forced to stay at the resort if a storm flooded the road or the bridges flooded out. "Everybody would get their food together and we had one big party," according to Aggie. Claire Walker says that following a barbecue after a board meeting, "I have one picture where we all piled on one of the king-size beds in one of the units, just for fun to have a picture of all of us." Lionel Medeiros and Mary Neudorffer held a jam-packed party at the pool the night before their wedding. "So we just took over the whole place, had a big, giant feed and all that. It was just great."

At the dinner to celebrate the annual owners' meeting in May 2002, our groups coordinator Mary McDerment organized a performance based on the film *Cabaret*. Mary also sang, reprising her role from the wedding of Laura and Tommy Richards. More recently, the marriage of Prince William and Kate Middleton was celebrated with a "fascinator" party. John Brekke participated fully. "I mean, that was over the top," John says. "They plugged a fascinator on me. I mean, it was just full sail, everything pulled!"

One evening in the Mediterranean Gourmet, following a spontaneous dinner gathering of about a dozen owners and staff, Averil Koch led a rousing full-throated chorus of "Goodnight Irene." Fortunately for the reputation of the restaurant, most of the other diners had already left for home.

Moreen and Chuck Williams recall that the pool was the location for an annual Thanksgiving by the Pool event. Chuck remembers:

> Oh, we used to do Thanksgiving by the pool. Everybody would bring something. We weren't owners yet. Our children are the ones that own the unit. But we were always guests. Every year, they would have a Thanksgiving dinner, everybody would bring something. Moreen got a recipe from Shelly's mother-in-law for bourbon sweet potato casserole. Every year, they'd ask me to make it. People really loved that, and actually, for many years since then, people would ask for the recipes, and when they were still doing the Thanksgiving dinners, it was like, well, "Can you bring the sweet potato recipe that you have?" Well, one year when we were here, Shelly and Mark were with us and I think Heidi was here, too. But we were all down here and they wanted the sweet potatoes. So the only grater we had in the room at that time was this little grater. We bought all these sweet potatoes and we had to send Mark out for more bourbon. We were running out of it. They used almost a fifth of bourbon. We made so much sweet potatoes for everybody. And we broke the grater.

Some events tended toward the spectacular. In January 2000, Rich and Nancee Sells organized a bicentennial party for fifty close friends and acquaintances. A local band performed, and there were fireworks. This was actually a blend of two parties, a massive Mai Tai Party for the owners at the pool and a centennial party at the restaurant. Anybody could come to the restaurant party. According to Laura Richards, "We had a huge band, we had a big dinner, and we had champagne glasses made special for everybody. It was just a huge, huge celebration. We had one owner who mysteriously brought fireworks and scared the you-know-what out of us."

On many occasions, grand dinners have been celebrated where all the owners and staff introduced their children, exchanged stories, and had a fine time together. Georgia Henry happily recalls:

> Owners' meetings were looked forward to quite a bit because you get involved and you become quite fond of some of them. I had parties in the pool area. Our gardener, Benny, was a chef at Princeville and a caterer. He did some beautiful things for our parties. We had local neighbors come in, and they did Hawaiian music. We had an owner who was Hawaiian, and he did a hula. Dusty Walker performed because that's what he did for a living. It was wonderful. We had good fun.

For Molly Ksander, these are important occasions during which "the whole HCR community would come together. Getting to know the people who worked there and their families, and connecting with them. It's more a family, *'ohana* feeling. We got to share and got to know the people that work there and take care of our home." A fine example of owners and staff getting together is a recent dinner where Cheryl Paogofie, a member of the housekeeping staff who was also the lead singer, organized the entertainment, consisting of local musicians and residents. Her preteen son performed with the band, and the kids of the performers and of the other staff that attended played with the owners. The Mediterranean Gourmet of course, provided food.

On the other hand, many a quiet dinner has also been shared, potlucks prepared by the participants themselves, where the entertainment is simply the satisfaction of being together. Claire Walker agrees. "We really had so much fun with the owners that have had properties here. It's so important for new owners, particularly, to feel welcome. And guests that stayed here loved it, too. We'd have a potluck together and sit around and talk stories, it's great."

The weekly Mai Tai Nights are like this—everyone brings their own offering for sharing with the others. Mai Tai Nights are an especially important opportunity for bringing guests into the HCR family. I will never forget two women who had discovered HCR by accident on a Mai Tai Night. Their eyes couldn't have gotten any wider. They couldn't have said, "Oh wow!" any more times. Molly Ksander also offers fond Mai Tai Night memories:

> Not so much the Mai Tai part of it, but just being in contact with people who have just arrived, new families, they've just come down the road, and it's a rainy, blustery night, or they've just discovered HCR and their kids are just delighted. I love to hear their tales of how they got there, and it reminds me of why I'm there.

Special events for the staff have long been celebrated, too. Recalling the early 1980s, Georgia Henry tells of "very happy meetings with the staff. They were potluck, and we had a couple of fantastic cooks among the maids. We just got together once in a great while and did that, and it was quite wonderful, involving all of our employees." Tommy Richards happily tells of "numerous birthday parties at the pool" and "staff meetings at the pool and at our house." He has "lots of memories with good people helping each other, celebrations, birthdays, kid birthdays, one-year baby birthdays. Lots of great memories." Christmas parties are especially remembered, sometimes with tents, disc jockeys, and light shows.

Major celebrations have marked historic and significant milestones. In 1969, the original owners celebrated the opening of the resort with a celebratory luncheon, the start of a long and storied tradition. Earlier, we saw the momentous celebration of the reopening following the Iniki reconstruction. There are others worthy of note. In 1999, HCR celebrated its thirtieth anniversary. This was a big event! There were three days of different types of Hawaiian celebrations. There was a big lu'au, and gifts were made for everyone. There was even a 30 percent discount to honor the thirtieth anniversary. Laura Richards and Candy Aluli organized preparation of a brochure describing the history of HCR to that point. Janne Hayward dug deep into her memories and archives to fill out the story of *Thirty Years of Aloha 1969–1999*. The celebration of HCR's fortieth anniversary in 2009 was more sedate than the thirtieth anniversary events. There was a prayer circle and an owners' dinner. There are only a few more years now to prepare for the glorious fiftieth anniversary celebration!

The very operation of HCR, as a condominium and as a resort business, is a community activity in which each member participates in one way or another. According to John Brekke,

> To me, something that is communal is, in some ways, more important to me than something that is individualistic. Part of the reason I love this place so much is because it's reminiscent to me of those experiences, communal experiences, 'ohana experiences. Well, I fell in love with the place just experiencing it and looking at it. Then, when I found out how it operated, I thought, *This is perfect*. Because we had been up to the Cliffs and it's all managed by individual owners. Everybody's competing for guests and advertising their own units. When I heard how this place operated, I thought, *This is aloha; this is 'ohana*. And I thought, *Not only is it the beauty of this island, but it's that collective beauty of how a place can run*.

It is clear here that John is referring to how the HCR rental program operates as a resort business. It is run as a community effort, where the owners work cooperatively for the joint benefit of the whole resort, rather than, as in most condominium projects, competing with each other to maximize their individual benefits. This not only strengthens community ties, but also, in a fundamental way, enables HCR to exist as a community, not just as a group of individuals.

HCR itself is a member of many communities. Among other things, it is part of Wainiha and Ha'ena. It is part of the north shore. And it is part of Kaua'i. Therefore, HCR has long participated in activities aimed at the wider welfare of these communities. In 1991, HCR participated in the annual Monk Seal Watch. This effort resulted in saving a monk seal pup called Kahina, or Hina for short, born during the event. HCR received a letter of thanks from the US Department of the Interior.

Following Iniki, HCR served as a drop-off point for dogs and cats that would then be taken to the Humane Society. All were placed in homes by the time HCR reopened. (The Hawai'i Humane Society later adopted the HCR method.) HCR volunteers helped with beach and trash pickup. The HCR community also pitched in to provide volunteers to assist in the creation and maintenance of the plantings at the Lihue Gateway Project, just outside the airport.

Over the years, HCR has supported a number of institutions and benevolent associations, several Kaua'i schools, the 4H Club, the Navy-Marine Corps Relief Fund, the Hawai'i International Film Festival, and the United Cerebral Palsy Charitable Auction, for example, often by contributing room stays to be used as prizes. HCR has regularly participated in the annual Kaua'i Charity Walk, provided volunteers to work at Limahuli Garden, participated in the Rotary Club's efforts to distribute lifesaving rescue tubes at beaches, and in 2013, participated in Rotary's project to renovate the Hanalei Pier. In 2014, HCR was participating in development of both the Ha'ena Master Plan, to protect the nature of the local community, and the Ha'ena Emergency Master Plan, to guide response in disasters.

Communities frequently form as a result of tragedy. Sometimes those communities can be remote and anonymous but nevertheless united by their shared humanity. In 1999, Bob Eckert was in Colorado, right across the street from Columbine High School at the time of the shootings. He recalled how someone had written in his guest book that HCR was a place of healing, so he decided that he would donate some of his unit time to the twelve families that lost a child and an adult who lost a spouse. Other owners also contributed time, so that in the end, thirteen weeks were donated, which was sufficient to cover all the families if they accepted the offer. Chris Bryan coordinated the program. It was agreed that no public announcement would be made, and that the effort would not be used to promote or publicize the resort. "They came anonymously," says Bob. "They just came to the healing power at Hanalei Colony Resort."

Think about the HCR people you have met. Scroll through your memories of doings with friends, family, neighbors. What is your fondest memory of HCR? It has people in it, doesn't it?

Chapter 12
A Special Place

If you talk to folks from HCR for even thirty seconds and ask what attracts them to HCR, their eyes get glassy, and their gaze lifts to focus on a distant vision. They will respond, "It's just such a...*special place!*" If you ask them what makes it so special, they will regain that distant look and respond with, "Many things!" HCR is special because of where it is, what it is, and how it came to be, and it is special because of its people, who they are, and how they came together. It is all these at once, each inseparable from the other, a whole that is much, much more than the sum of its parts.

HCR is special because of where it is. HCR is set in a place of vivid natural beauty, a feast for the senses. Nature seems to encompass everything. The colors are intense and changing. You can see the surroundings, the sea, the sky, the trees, and the mountains between the buildings, reflected in windows and even shining through sets of windows. It is as though the natural landscape permeates the built landscape and incorporates it. The visual textures give you the sense that your fingers can feel the surface of the mountain forest and the lava rock. HCR is not really silent, but it seems to be because usually the only sounds you hear are the sounds of nature, the underlying constant rumble and hiss of the surf, and the occasional tweeting of birds. There is a blend of fragrances—plumeria, gardenia, the smell of the sea. HCR is special because it is an exceptional spot in an extraordinary landscape. A distinct spirit of place inhabits this spot and this setting, a spirit that projects seclusion, peace, and contentment. And it is special because it is on the north shore. On Kaua'i. In Hawai'i.

HCR is special because of what it is. HCR is not just a home or a hideaway or a source of income or a gathering place. HCR is all these things, and it is special precisely because it is all these things. They reinforce each other. For owners and guests, HCR may be home for many months at a time or for just a few days. Everything is familiar, and everything is the same, the way it should be, the way they like it, with the people they like. Everything they need is nearby. There is no need to work, to worry. HCR shelters its people from the world, and it restores them. It offers rest, and it offers recreation. It offers entertainment, fun, and adventure for body and mind. HCR is special because it is home and not home, simultaneously relaxing and exciting, healing and stimulating.

HCR is special because of how it came to be. HCR has a unique and extraordinary history; a distinctive, centuries-long transition from its past to its present; and a story of its fragile relationship with the threatening forces of nature, its continued evolution to meet the changing needs of its people, and its search for the future. HCR is special because of the tales of the spirits and the ancestors who dwelled here, the work of the *maka'ainana* and ali'i who lived here, the visions of its architects and builders, the hazards of nature, the determination of its restorers, and the devotion of its people. HCR is special because of its unique past that binds myth, legend, history, and memory.

HCR is special because of how its people came together. HCR has schemed to cast its magic spell that first attracted and then captivated the people who give it life. It is special because of the unique concatenations of chance, love at first sight, spontaneous decisions, magic enticements, blind sight, and compulsion that it has used to lure and capture its people. It is special because of all the paths that, started where they may and twisted where they might, converged to bring HCR's family together.

HCR is special because of its people. HCR is special because of all the people who have lived here of old, who have built HCR, and who work here and dwell here now—HCR's extended family. The people of the HCR community complement the beauty of the place. HCR is special because of the many people who contributed to creating it and shaping and preserving its present form, and who work to ensure its continued flourishing. Most certainly HCR is special because of those who continue to live and work at HCR—a little or a lot—and love it and show new generations of staff, guests, and family how to love it. HCR is special because it is the thing that binds this rich diversity of people into a single community, an *'ohana nui* that forms its soul.

To create something is first to experience it in a new way, a unique way, and then to pass it on to others so that they, too, experience the thing in a new way, so that it changes the way others experience the thing. It is to connect things that were separate before, things like beauty, locale, environment, family, history, legends, and community. People go to HCR to find…many things. They have found them. More importantly, in that finding, they have created something new, something unique, something extraordinary. They have created HCR. This is how it came to be. This is why Hanalei Colony Resort is special.

Chapter 13

Departing

The air is still. You are on your lanai, gazing at the wide horizon, the uniform gray of the sky merging with the flat gray of the sea. The mountains are disappearing in mist. A storm is coming in from the other side of the island. You back off the lanai, leaving the curtains open; you turn to leave, then glance back through the window once more. You lock the door and leave your apartment, suitcase in hand. A brilliant white egret glides in and settles slowly on the ironwood hedge. Following the path past the ti and croton and spider lily plantings, you pause once more to gaze at the horizon between the buildings, across the big green lawn through the ironwood trees. You drop your keys at the cottage, load your car, and leave the lot, passing again beneath the coconut palms and Cook pines. Beyond the naupaka hedge, the sea is calm, and the sky is ominous.

Leaving the parking lot, you turn left, past the red hibiscus, away from the beach toward the bridges, toward the town, toward the beginning of the road. You wind back through Wainiha, across the bridges, up the slope on the narrow, twisting road on the cliff, looking back across the bay, perhaps with a tear in your eye. Ahead, in the east, the sky lightens up; the clouds are opening. You look back—one last time—across the water. The sun has broken through, and there is a rainbow across the bay—a double rainbow. Through the arch, HCR glows in the light. It will be waiting: Unspoiled. Unplugged. Unforgettable. You will return. HCR will never be far from your heart and mind.

A hui hou! Until we meet again.

Glossary

(The definitions given here are drawn principally, but not exclusively, from M. K. Pukui and S. H. Elbert.)

A hui hou	Until we meet again, good-bye
Ahupua'a	Land division usually extending from the uplands to the sea, often a river valley and its drainage system
'Aina	Land, earth
Ali'i	Chief or chiefess
Aloha	Love, affection; "Greetings!"; "Farewell!"
'Awa	Kava, local pepper plant, the root being the source of a narcotic drink of the same name used in ceremonies
Hala	Pandanus tree
Halau	Institution for learning hula; long house, as for hula instruction
Hale	House, building
Hanai	Foster child, adopted child
Hau	Sea hibiscus tree
He'e	Octopus

Heiau	Pre-Christian place of worship
Hoa'aina	Tenant, caretaker, as on a kuleana
Hui	Club, association, corporation, organization; joint ownership, usually of land
Hukilau	A seine net; to fish with a seine net; community fishing event
Kahuna	Priest, expert in any profession
Kama'aina	Native-born
Kapa	Tapa, cloth made from paper mulberry (*wauke*) plant
Kapu	Taboo, prohibition; sacred
Keiki	Child
Konohiki	Headman of an ahupua'a under the chief
Kula	Field, open country, pasture
Kuleana	Small piece of property awarded to individuals in the *Mahele*; responsibility
Lanai	Porch, veranda, balcony
Lu'au	Feast
Lei	Garland, wreath; necklace of flowers, leaves, shells, ivory, or paper
Lo'i	Irrigated terrace, especially for taro

Luna nui	Chief officer or foreman, superintendent
Mahalo nui loa	"Thank you very much"
Mahele	The legal process begun in 1848 to divide, share, and privatize the land among the king, chiefs, and people
Mai tai	A rum drink
Mahimahi	A game fish popular for food
Maka'ainana	Populace, citizen
Makai	Toward the sea
Mauka	Inland
Mo'i	King
Mo'o	Lizard, dragon, water spirit
Mu'umu'u	Loose gown
Nui	Big, great
'Oahi	Fireworks
'Ohana	Family, kin group
'Ohana nui	Extended family
Paniolo	Cowboy
Pau hana	Quitting time from work

Pilikia	Trouble
Pua	Flower
Pune'e	Movable couch
Pupu	Appetizer, hors d'oeuvre
Tapa	Kapa, cloth made from paper mulberry (*wauke*) plant
Taro (Kalo)	Plant of the Arum family used for food; its root is made into poi

Sources

Articles and Books

Andrade, Carlos. *Ha'ena: Through the Eyes of the Ancestors*. Honolulu: University of Hawai'i Press, 2008.

Anonymous. "Securing the Wainiha Water-Right Lease," in *Hawaiian Almanac and Annual for 1924* (Honolulu: Thos. G. Thrum, 1923), 95–112.

Anonymous. "The Benefits of Ahupua'a Are Taking Root in Present-Day Hawai'i," in Hawai'i Magazine (Honolulu: PacificBasin Communications, May/June 2013), 44.

Beckwith, Martha. *Hawaiian Mythology*. Honolulu: University of Hawai'i Press, 1940.

Cook, Chris and David Boynton. *The New Kaua'i Movie Book*. Honolulu: Mutual Publishing, LLC, 2013.

Cozad, Stormy. *Kauai: 100 Years in Postcards*. Charleston: Arcadia Publishing, 2011.

Daws, Gavan. *Shoal of Time: A History of the Hawaiian Islands*. Honolulu: University of Hawai'i Press, 1968.

Dye, Kekapala P. and Thomas S. Dye. "An Archeological Survey for Animal Control Fencing in the Wainiha Preserve, Wainiha Valley, Kaua'i." Report prepared for The Nature Conservancy, Kilauea, 2010.

Dye, Thomas S. "Archeological Assessment for a Residential Lot at Ha'ena, Kaua'i (TMK:5-9-02:62)," Report prepared for Marilyn M. Browning, Calabasas, 2002.

———. "Cultural Impacts Assessment of a Coastal Lot, (TMK:(4)5-9-05:029), at Ha'ena, Halele'a, Kaua'i." Report prepared for Landmark Consulting Services, Inc., Honolulu, 2005.

Earle, Timothy. *Economic and Social Organization of a Complex Chiefdom: The Halele'a District, Kaua'i, Hawaii.* Anthropological Papers, Museum of Anthropology, University of Michigan No. 63. Ann Arbor: Regents of the University of Michigan, The Museum of Anthropology, 1978.

Gartley, A. "Wainiha Electric Power Plant," in *Hawaiian Almanac and Annual for 1908* (Honolulu: Thos. G. Thrum, 1907), 141–56.

Griffin, P. Bion. "Where Lohi'au Ruled: Excavations at Ha'ena, Halele'a, Kaua'i." *Hawaiian Archeology 1* (1984), 1–17.

Harrington, Daniel. *Hanalei: A Kaua'i River Town.* Honolulu: Mutual Publishing, LLC, 2008.

Joesting, Edward. *Kauai: The Separate Kingdom.* Honolulu: University of Hawai'i Press, 1984.

Kame'eleihiwa, Lilikala. *Native Land and Foreign Desires: Pehea La E Pono Ai?* Honolulu: Bishop Museum Press, 1992.

Kanahele, George S. *Hawaiian Music and Musicians: An Illustrated History.* Honolulu: University of Hawai'i Press, 1979.

Kauai Historical Society. *The Kauai Papers.* Lihue: Kauai Historical Society, 1991.

Lydgate, Rev. John M. "The Affairs of the Wainiha Hui," in *Hawaiian Almanac and Annual for 1913* (Honolulu: Thos. G. Thrum, 1912), 125–37.

Puku'i, Mary Kawena and Caroline Curtis. *Tales of the Menehune.* Revised Edition. Honolulu: The Kamehameha Schools, 1985.

Pukui, Mary Kawena and Samuel H. Elbert. *Hawaiian Dictionary.* Revised and Enlarged Edition. Honolulu: University of Hawai'i Press, 1986.

Schütz, Albert J. *All About Hawaiian. A Kolowalu Book.* Honolulu: University of Hawai'i Press, 1995.

Stauffer, Robert H. *Kahana: How the Land Was Lost.* Honolulu: University of Hawai'i Press, 2004.

Wehrheim, John. *Taylor Camp.* Chicago: Serindia Publications, 2004.

Wichman, Frederick B. *Kauai Tales.* Honolulu: Bamboo Ridge Press, 1985.

———. *More Kaua'i Tales.* Honolulu: Bamboo Ridge Press, 1997.

———. *Kaua'i: Ancient Place-Names and Their Stories.* Honolulu: University of Hawai'i Press, 1998.

Websites

County of Kaua'i property record search: http://www.qpublic.net/hi/kauai/search.html

The *Garden Island* newspaper archives: http://thegardenisland.com/search/

HawaiiHistory.org: A community learning center: http://www.hawaiihistory.org/

Ivy Nishimoto: http://ivysplace.com/our-history

Kaua'i Historical Society: http://kauaihistoricalsociety.org/

Kaua'i Museum: http://www.kauaimuseum.org/

Library of Congress: Chronicling America: Historic Newspapers: http://chroniclingamerica.loc.gov/

Limahuli Garden and Preserve: History: http://ntbg.org/gardens/limahuli-history.php

Pacific Worlds: Welcome to Ha'ena. http://www.pacificworlds.com/haena/index.cfm

State of Hawai'i Department of Land and Natural Resources–Bureau of Conveyances, Land Title Records Online Search and Ordering System: https://boc.ehawaii.gov/docsearch/nameSearch.html

Ulukau: The Hawaiian Electronic Library: http://www.ulukau.org/

Wainiha Nation Blog: http://www.wainihanation.com/

Made in the USA
San Bernardino, CA
14 February 2015